A Friendly Guide to PRAYER

MICHAEL WHELAN SM

Dedicated to
Adrian van Kaam CSSp

My thanks to
Sr Marie Biddle RSJ and Ms Cathy Holling

Published by
John Garratt Publishing
32 Glenvale Crescent
Mulgrave Vic 3170 Australia
www.johngarratt.com.au

Copyright ©2011 Michael Whelan

All rights reserved. Except as provided by the Australian copyright law, no part of this book may be reproduced in any way without permission in writing from the publisher.

Design and typesetting by Lynne Muir
Text editing by Ann M Philpott
Photographs from www.thinkstockphotos.com.au

Cataloguing-in-Publication information for this title is available from the National Library of Australia. www.nla.gov.au

ISBN 9781921946141

Nihil Obstat : Reverend Gerard Diamond MA (Oxon), LSS, D Theol Diocesan Censor
Imprimatur : Most Reverend Les Tomlinson DD Titular Bishop of Siniti, Vicar General
Date : 26 October 2011

The Nihil Obstat and Imprimatur are official declarations that a book or pamphlet is free of doctrinal or moral error. No implication is contained therein that those who have granted the Nihil Obstat and Imprimatur agree with the contents, opinions or statements expressed. They do not necessarily signify that the work is approved as a basic text for catechetical instruction.

Scripture quotations are drawn from the *New Revised Standard Version of the Bible*, copyright ©1989 by the Division of Christian Education of the National Council of the Churches of Christ in the USA. Used by permission. All rights reserved. Excerpt from pp. 121-122 of Thomas Keating's *Open Mind, Open Heart* reproduced by kind permission of Continuum International Publishing Group.

Contents

Foreword...5

Introduction...7

1. Mystery...9

2. "I AM WHO I AM"...12

3. "I will be with you"...15

4. The Kingdom is within...19

5. Liturgy...22

6. The inner journey...25

7. There are many ways...28

8. The body...32

9. The mind...36

10. The imagination...40

11. The emotions...43

12. Simplicity...47

13. A moral life...51

14. Discipline...54

15. Some Catholic practices...58

Endnotes 63

Deep listening opens us to the Presence everywhere.

Foreword

There are many stories coming from the Desert Fathers and Mothers of the third and fourth centuries. One of those stories concerns a learned man who came to Anthony, the greatest of the desert dwellers. He asked Anthony how he could endure living in the desert, deprived of the consolation of books. Anthony said: "My book, philosopher, is the nature of created things, and whenever I wish I can read in it the works of God."[1]

Anthony has put his finger on a central fact of Catholic spirituality: in the finite we meet the Infinite, in the human we meet the Divine and in the present we meet the Presence. God is everywhere and wherever God *is*, God *does* and God's doing is *loving* and God's loving is *liberating*.

This is for us both gift and task. First of all it is gift. We begin with what God has done, is doing and will continue to do. What is on offer is God's loving and liberating Presence, all the time, in all things, everywhere. Secondly it is task. We respond. Most fundamentally, this means waking up, becoming aware of what is going on throughout the cosmos, in the very depths of our beings, in each and every moment, in every person, event and thing. In Luke's Gospel we read:

> Be dressed for action and have your lamps lit; be like those who are waiting for their master to return from the wedding banquet, so that they may open the door for him as soon as he comes and knocks. (Lk 12:35-37)

Paradoxically, waking up – and perhaps more importantly, *staying awake* – requires constant and consistent work. It is an ongoing task. That task is by way of facilitation rather than mastery:

> Spiritual formation cannot be forced, only prepared for. Hence its means cannot be those of conquest, but only of facilitation and preparation.[2]

In the middle of the sixth century, the great monk, St Benedict – founder of the Benedictine orders – gives us some very helpful advice. The first word in his *Rule* is "Listen!" A little further on St Benedict adds: "Listen with the ear of the heart." Deep listening opens us to the Presence everywhere.

Here we are at the heart of prayer as it is understood within the Catholic Tradition. It is the way we will speak of prayer throughout this book – *being present to the Presence*. Our focus will therefore be primarily on attitudes and dispositions rather than specific acts and rituals. It is the prayerful person we are most interested in, rather than the person who says prayers, the prayerful life rather than the life that contains times of prayer. We must of course pay some attention to specific acts and rituals, prayers and times of prayer. These have a very important place in the Catholic Tradition. They, however, will be discussed as the servants and instruments of the prayerful person and the prayerful life.

The tradition of prayer within the Catholic Church is rich, varied and complex. There are many people, themes, practices and sources that could be usefully studied. We could also address many specific problems that arise. A much larger book would be required to do all that.

As a reader of this book you will hopefully find at least three things:

sufficient substance and clarity in the material presented to enable you to begin to understand something – or deepen your understanding – of the enormous riches and complexity of prayer within the Catholic Tradition

enough practical guidance to enable you to begin – or perhaps simply refine and deepen – your practice of prayer

encouragement to go on exploring the possibilities in prayer for you personally, for your family and friends, and for the wider community.

Let me suggest finally that this book is best read slowly. The act of reading can be a prayerful act and a deepening of your prayerfulness. Together we shall try to go as deep as we possibly can. We cannot do that at speed. Slow down, clear your mind of distractions. Pay close attention to both what the text on the page is saying and what the text in your own heart is saying. Heed the advice of the poet:

> He (she) does not always remain bent over his pages; he (she) often leans back and closes his (her) eyes over a line he (she) has been reading again, and its meaning spreads through his (her) blood.[3]

Michael Whelan SM PhD

Introduction

If we were to gather one hundred Catholics in a room and ask them to write down what they think prayer is, we would no doubt get a variety of responses. And they might all be in some sense "right". The various responses might emphasise conversation, the heart, petition, praise, contemplation, rituals, grace, God, attentiveness, silence or perhaps a number of the above, or something else.

However, we could expect every response to imply, if not explicitly state, that prayer is fundamentally about *presence* – our presence with God and God's Presence with us. Before prayer is a method or action or word or ritual, it is a response to the Presence of God.

Presence implies relationship. In fact, being present – *really present* – is simply a way of emphasising that the relationship is more or less focused and attentive. It is possible, for example, to be standing next to someone but not be really present to that person. Similarly, it is possible to be really present to someone on the other side of the world.

Human presence is more about the inner world than the physical or visible world. To speak of presence implies that the relationship has some depth to it, some connection with our inner world and who and what we actually are as human beings.

Being prayerful goes to the heart of what it means to be human. Relationships are the very essence of being human. There is nothing you can say of yourself that does not bear some relationship to someone or something beyond yourself. Our humanity is constituted in and through relationship:

> Relationship is, then, written into the very nature of the human person. As the Bible sees human beings, you cannot think about the person without recognizing that he or she is, as it were, made for relationship.[4]

Relationship is fourfold. The first expression of relationship, the one that gives context and meaning to all the others, is the relationship with God, however we name God. The second expression of relationship is with oneself, the third with other people and the fourth with the events and things of our lives. In a healthy life, all four expressions of relationship thrive, more or less.

It is an axiom of the Catholic Tradition that we find ourselves – our *true self* – in God. When that relationship with God is growing alive and active, when we are awakening to the liberating truth of it, all else – our longings, fears, anxieties, hopes, joys, sadnesses, achievements, frustrations – find a relative place there. In the context of that relationship, all else can be faced and experienced as promise rather than as threat.

Disconnected from that transcendent context, things tend to lose their proper perspective. Some things we exaggerate out of proportion; others we diminish or even overlook. Means easily become ends, ends easily become means, the relative things can become absolutised and the Absolute can become relativised or lost sight of altogether. When our particular social environment is suffering from such disconnection, people may look askance at someone who has woken up to what is going on and has begun to live in accord with this awakened state. Again we can turn to the Desert Father St Anthony for practical advice:

> A time is coming when people will go mad and when they meet someone who is not mad, they will turn to them and say, "You are out of your mind," just because they are not like them.[5]

The prayerful person is one who is more or less present to the Presence in each moment, in all people, in all events and things, everywhere. This is enabled and promoted by study and acts and habits that support listening and attentiveness to what is happening – what is *really happening* – in and around us.

When we are present to the Presence, we are more likely to be truly present to ourselves, others and the events and things of our world. And vice versa, when we are truly present to ourselves, others and the events and things of our world, we are more likely to be present to the Presence.

Culture and society can create a thicket of unreality. Our own anxieties, fears, selfishness and greed can contribute to this thicket of unreality. Perhaps more importantly, our own particular inclinations to self-deception – and we are all geniuses at self-deception – can incline us to sleepwalk through life, never taking stock, never waking up to what is actually happening in and around us.

The prayerful person is the awakened person. The prayerful life is the awakened life. As both cause and effect of the awakening, we are willing and able to listen and hear and face what is happening.

This is in fact another way of thinking of our deepest possibilities as human beings. It is about turning up for life wide awake. It is a journey into our own humanity. And the ultimate discovery that awaits us – the ultimate *experience* that awaits us – is that this very journey into our humanity is also a journey into Divinity.

How often can we say we are fully present to God or to ourselves or to others or to any event or thing? And in those rare moments when we are fully present, are they not also the moments when we glimpse in some small way what it is to be truly alive?

> The prayerful person is one who is more or less present to the Presence in each moment, in all people, in all events and things, everywhere.

1
Mystery

Life is a mystery to be lived, not a problem to be solved.[6]

Problems are challenges to our cleverness, ingenuity, endurance and skills. Problems have solutions, at least in principle. If we are clever enough, work hard enough and have the right tools, problems give way to solutions. Solutions, in turn, bring closure and closure brings a sense of power, and power brings a sense of control. All of which is entirely appropriate if we are dealing with machines or merely functional issues.

Our daily experience, however, reminds us repeatedly that there is no solution to life as such. Life is much more than a problem or even a series of problems. It is that "more than" that calls for serious attention. There is always more to discover, more to deal with, more to enjoy, more to suffer, more to live, and more to wonder about. Every moment contains the rider: "There is more than this!" The "more than" confronts us everywhere, in every moment. In fact, our daily experience brings us face to face with an *inexhaustible intelligibility* in and around us. We can know and understand so much, but not all. The possibilities are inexhaustible. The more we know, the more we know we do not know. Every answer brings with it more questions.

Together with the discovery of the inexhaustible intelligibility in our lives comes the discovery of *ultimate uncontrollability*. Daily living contains constant reminders of our limits. The older we get the more obvious are these reminders. Again, it is inconceivable that the human family would ever reach the stage where everything was literally under control. Life will always be full of surprises, for better or worse. We will never exhaust the intelligibility of the world, nor will we ever be rid of our limits.

We call this *mystery*. Yes, life contains a multitude of problems that cry out for solutions. But more importantly, life is a mystery that must be lived. The problem-solving approach is good when we are dealing with problems. A different response – something much deeper – is required when we are dealing with mystery. Mystery calls for an attentive, listening response, and for trust and submission. Mystery – when we respond well – evokes humility and awe, reverence and gratitude, surrender and contemplation.

The more deeply we live our lives, the less helpful and the more destructive, in fact, is the problem-solving approach. For example, consider a work of art or moments of playfulness, a loving relationship, being with someone who is grieving or the moment of simply turning up for a new day with a measure of good will. There will normally be problems attendant upon such things or moments because problems and mystery are intermingled and intertwined in our daily lives. But the heart of such things or moments must not be treated as a problem. Such things and moments usher us into the presence of mystery. How well we respond will have a significant bearing on how well we live as human beings.

When we are faced with a problem the correct question is, "What can/must I *do*?" When we are faced with mystery the correct question is, "What *attitude* must I develop?" Here we are on the human ground of prayerfulness and the prayerful life. Our Catholic Tradition urges us to listen attentively to the promptings of the human heart at this point. Those promptings will point us in the direction of the Great Mystery beyond the ordinary mystery of our days.

For reflection

Take each text on its own and read it slowly and reflectively. Listen with the ear of the heart. Pause from time to time and listen to any movement within, whether it be a movement of resonance or resistance. Let the process lead you to some kind of words with God.

This life is much too much trouble, far too strange, to arrive at the end of it and then be asked what you make of it and have to answer, 'Scientific humanism.' That won't do. A poor show. Life is a mystery, love is a delight. Therefore I take it as axiomatic, that one should settle for nothing less than the infinite mystery and the infinite delight; i.e. God. In fact, I demand it. I refuse to settle for anything less. I don't see why anyone should settle for anything less than Jacob, who actually grabbed aholt of God and wouldn't let go until God identified himself and blessed him.[7]

The heart has its reasons, of which reason knows nothing; we feel it in many things. I say that the soul naturally loves universal being, and naturally loves itself according as it devotes itself thereto; and it hardens itself against one or the other as it pleases.[9]

Very gradually we learn the crucial lesson of existence, that we do not ask what life has to give to us, but rather respond to what life asks from us. Then the question is no longer what can I get out of life, but rather what can life get out of me.[8]

Christianity in its true essence is the state of radical openness to the question of the mystery of the Absolute Future which is God. All individual statements in Christianity, in its knowledge and life, can be understood only as a modality of this radical commitment to refuse to call a halt at any point and to seek the fulfillment of its life, its 'salvation,' in something to which no further name can be assigned.[10]

For practice

Our days are filled with many things we generally do with little or no reflection – opening or closing a door, making a cup of coffee, folding bed sheets, walking along the street, washing our face, ironing, turning a light switch on and so on. This week, make a point of becoming present to yourself as you do these things. Slow down. Become aware rather than deliberate. Listen with the ear of the heart, be attuned to what is happening. You are actually a participant in something bigger than yourself. There is grace in each and every moment, each and every event.

2
"I am who I am"

"Moses said to God, 'If I come to the Israelites and say to them, 'The God of your ancestors has sent me to you,' and they ask me, 'What is his name?' what shall I say to them?' God said to Moses, 'I AM WHO I AM.'"(Ex 3:13-14)

A Jewish author notes that "it is stated in the Talmud, 'And God said unto Moses... This is My name for ever' (Ex 3:15). The Hebrew word 'for ever' (*leolam*) is written here in a way that it may be read *lealem* which means 'to conceal.' The name of God is to be concealed."[11] Thus the Sovereign Mystery of God is protected. This Mystery is the Source of that mystery which is signalled in our daily lives by the experiences of inexhaustible intelligibility and ultimate uncontrollability. The mystery we encounter in every moment and in each person, event or thing is but a dim reflection of the Mystery revealed to us under the enigmatic name, "I AM WHO I AM" (YHWH) (Ex 3:12).

St Thomas Aquinas says, "it is impossible for any created intellect to comprehend God."[12] St Thomas then goes on to say that even "by the revelation of grace we cannot know of God *what he is*, and thus are united to him as one unknown".[13] St Augustine writes similarly: "If you are able to understand what you are saying about God, it is not God."[14]

The Catholic Tradition recognises a deep tension – one that can be very constructive – between what we can know and understand and say about God on the one hand and what we cannot know and understand and say on the other hand. We refer to these two ways of approaching God as the *kataphatic way* and the *apophatic way*.

The *kataphatic way* says there are some meaningful affirmations we can – indeed must – say of God. Thus we say, "God exists" and "God is love". Such affirmations say something valid and meaningful. This is sometimes referred to as the *via positive*, "the positive way" or "the way of affirmation". As we explore the possibilities and limits of the *kataphatic way*, we are soon struck by the awful inadequacy of human understanding and speech before the Infinite. It is here that the inexhaustible intelligibility hits us forcefully. Openness of mind and silence of speech is a good response. Thus the *apophatic way* is a necessary complement to the *kataphatic way*.

The Greek roots kata, meaning "thoroughly" or "entirely", and phanai, meaning "speak", combine to form the term kataphasis, which means "affirmation". Conversely, the Greek root apo, meaning "from" or "away", and therefore some kind of negation or breakdown, combines with phanai to form the term apophasis, which means "denial" or "breakdown/failure of speech". An irony is implied here: we must speak of God in order to find that point at which speech fails.

The *apophatic way* says we must protect the ultimate incomprehensibility and unknowability of God by going beyond all affirmations when we speak of God. Thus we say, "God is more than we could ever possibly understand by using the word 'exist'" and "God is more than what we could ever possibly understand by using the word 'love'." This is sometimes referred to as the *via negative*, "the negative way" or "the way of negation".

The *apophatic way* keeps saying "No!" to the claims of the *kataphatic way* and the latter keeps struggling with its claims anyway. We could say that the *apophatic way* guards the otherness and transcendence of God while the *kataphatic way* guards the intimacy and immanence of God.

St Thomas Aquinas bears witness to the integration of both ways. His writings are an excellent example of meaningful and rich affirmations concerning God and our relationship with God. Yet, towards the end of his life, he is reputed to have said that all he had written was "so much straw" compared with the reality he knew to be there.

For reflection

Take each text on its own and read it slowly and reflectively. Listen with the ear of the heart. Pause from time to time and listen to any movement within, whether it be a movement of resonance or resistance. Let the process lead you to some kind of words with God then perhaps silence.

"Scripture teaches that religious knowledge comes at first to those who receive it as light. … But as the mind progresses and, through an ever greater and even more perfect diligence, comes to apprehend reality, as it approaches more nearly to contemplation, it sees more clearly what of the divine nature is uncontemplated. For leaving behind everything that is observed, not only what sense comprehends but also what the intelligence thinks it sees, it keeps on penetrating deeper until by the intelligence's yearning for understanding it gains access to the invisible and the incomprehensible, and there it sees God. This is the true knowledge of what is sought; this is the seeing that consists in not seeing, because that which is sought transcends all knowledge, being separated on all sides by incomprehensibility as by a kind of darkness. Wherefore John the sublime, who penetrated into the luminous darkness, says, 'No one has ever seen God,' thus asserting that knowledge of the divine essence is unattainable not only by men but also by every intelligent creature."[15]

"It is he alone who has immortality and dwells in unapproachable light, whom no one has ever seen or can see; to him be honor and eternal dominion. Amen." (1 Tim 6:16)

"Do not place your happiness in what you can hear or feel of God in prayer but rather in what you can neither feel nor understand. God is always hidden and difficult to find. Go on serving God in this way, as though God were concealed in a sacred place, even when you think you have found God, felt God or heard God. The less you understand, the closer you get to God. Prayer will show you that God is forever the Wholly Other, and you will always fall short.

Prayer will teach you, too, that God is nearer to you than you are to yourself. After passing the fiery crucible and stepping through the narrow doorway where you can bring nothing with you, enter the cave of your heart that contains God, whom the universe cannot hold.

In prayer, then, you will find *peace, light and joy*. There will be the source of your love and the strength of your life. To enlighten your mind, pray. To discern your path, pray. To unify your being, pray … That light may fall on your face and rejoice your heart, pray. To be incorporated into Christ, pray; you no longer live but Christ lives in you. Gradually you will be enlightened, cleansed, purified, matured and joyfully quickened. And so, deified. Filled with your fullness you will be able to enter God's total plenitude. Nothing is left but to contemplate God's glory."[16]

For practice

Towards the end of the *Spiritual Exercises* of St Ignatius of Loyola, there is a well-known prayer: "Take O Lord and receive my entire liberty, my memory, my understanding, my whole will. All that I am, and all that I possess you have given me. I surrender it all to you to be disposed of according to your most holy will. Give me only your love and your grace. With these I will be rich enough and will desire nothing more." Repeat this prayer each day over the coming month. And listen to what is happening within you as you pray the prayer.

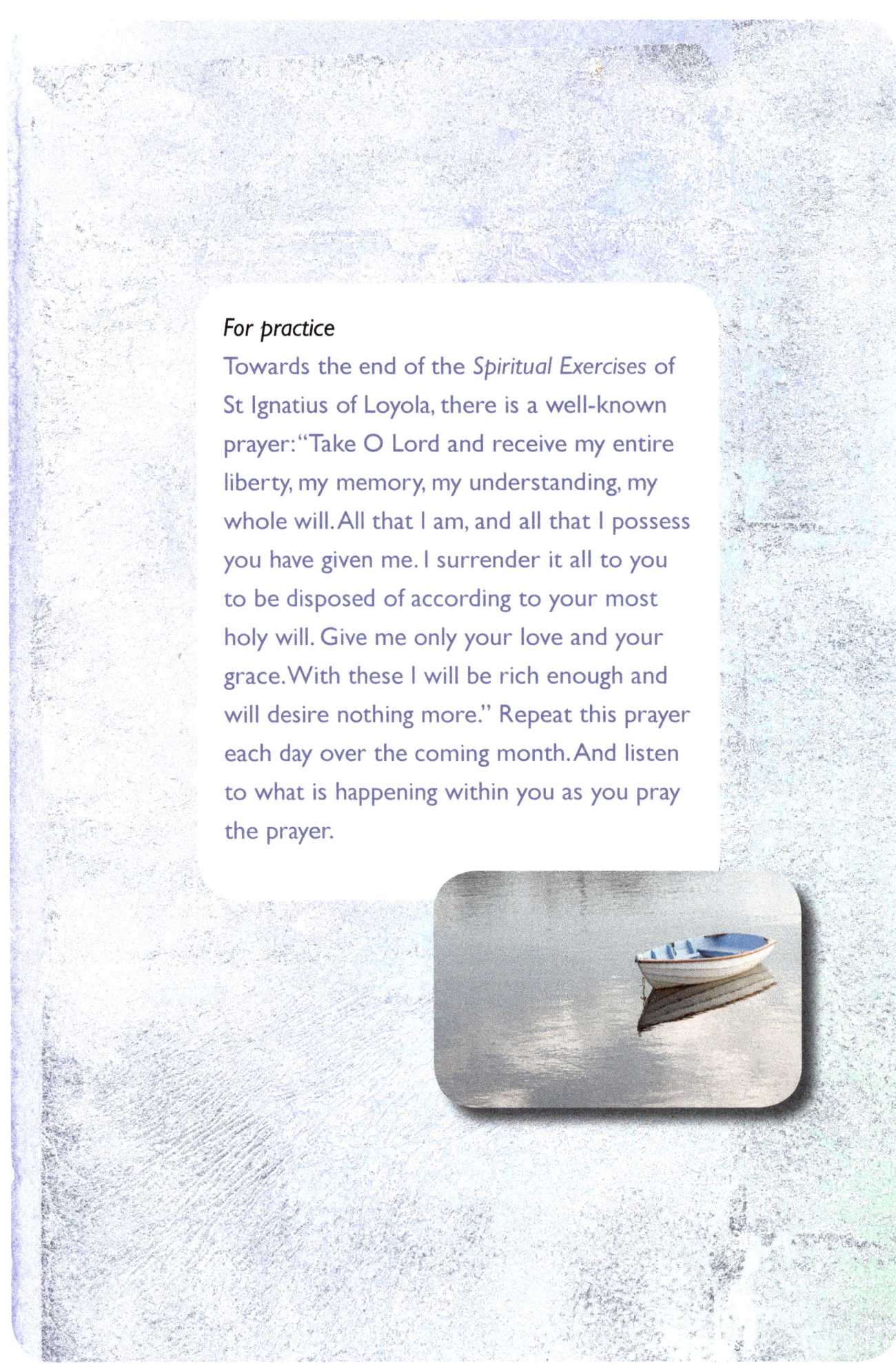

3
"I will be with you"

"The text (Ex 3:1–15) ... contains a threefold revelation – of God's immanence in history, of his transcendence to history, and of his transparence through history. God first asserts the fact of his presence in the history of his people: 'I shall be there'. Second, he asserts the mystery of his own being: 'I shall be there as who I am'. His mystery is a mode of absence. Third, he asserts that, despite his absence in mystery, he will make himself known to his people: 'As who I am shall I be there.'"[17]

A few lines before the text revealing the Name (see Ex 3:15) is the promise: "I will be with you" (Ex 3:12). The two revelations – "I AM WHO I AM" and "I will be with you" – belong together. The mere revelation of the Name does not necessarily imply any significant connection with Moses and the people; it says nothing explicit about relationship or presence. It reveals the transcendence of God, not God's immanence. The two revelations together assure us that the Mystery is *both* transcendent *and* immanent, utterly other *and* utterly intimate, transcending history *and* active in history, independent of us *and* irrevocably for us.

Jesus of Nazareth is the Sovereign Mystery enfleshed. In the Greek version of the Jewish Bible, the word *Kyrios* ("Lord") is used to translate the "I AM WHO I AM". The followers of Jesus use this same Greek word *Kyrios* ("Lord") to speak of Jesus – "Jesus is Lord!" (see, for example, 1 Cor 12:3 and Rom 10:9).

Jesus embodies the twofold revelation of transcendence and immanence. The Gospel of Matthew goes so far as to explicitly identify Jesus with the Emmanuel of Isaiah 7:14, noting that the name means "God-with-us" (Mt 1:26). For St Paul, we find in Jesus Christ the presence of "the mystery hidden in all ages". (Eph 3:9)

The story of Jesus' passion, death and resurrection in each of the Gospels is the ultimate revelation of the Sovereign Mystery acting for us. We refer to this action of God in Jesus of Nazareth as the *Paschal Mystery*. The word "paschal" comes from the Hebrew word *pesah* which means "Passover". This central feast of Passover in the Jewish calendar, when a lamb is sacrificed to ritually recall God's liberating action in the Exodus Event, became the key for the early Christian community in understanding what God had done in Jesus. John's Gospel declares quite explicitly: "Look there is the lamb of God!" (Jn 1:29).

In each Gospel the Cross and the empty tomb are the symbols of God's victory in Jesus. The outcome of that victory is the Kingdom, a state of being in which unity and peace, truth and goodness, and love and forgiveness have the final say.

St Paul writes: "All of us who have been baptized into Christ Jesus have been baptized into his death" (Rom 6:3). In Christ we are one with the Sovereign Mystery; we find our identity in

15

and through that Mystery. So St Paul prays for his brothers and sisters in Ephesus:

> I pray that, according to the riches of his glory, he may grant that you may be strengthened in your inner being with power through his Spirit, and that Christ may dwell in your hearts through faith, as you are being rooted and grounded in love. I pray that you may have the power to comprehend, with all the saints, what is the breadth and length and height and depth, and to know the love of Christ that surpasses knowledge, so that you may be filled with all the fullness of God. Now to him who by the power at work within us is able to accomplish abundantly far more than all we can ask or imagine, to him be glory in the church and in Christ Jesus to all generations, forever and ever. Amen. (Eph 3:16-21)

The Paschal Mystery is the life-giving centre of Christian prayer. The Paschal Mystery is the source of unity and community. St Paul is very clear in stating the depths of this unity and community: "It is no longer I who live, but it is Christ who lives in me" (Gal 2:20).

For reflection

Take each text on its own and read it slowly and reflectively. Listen with the ear of the heart. Pause from time to time and listen to any movement within, whether it be a movement of resonance or resistance. Let the process lead you to some kind of words with God. Perhaps you could do some more study on a theme emerging from your reflection.

"The Apostles never speak of a death that is anything but the one narrow gate to a new life. Why? Because if Christ has simply died on the Cross, Christianity falls to pieces. The whole foundation of the faith is the Resurrection, not merely as a strong 'apologetic argument,' but above all in the sense that it is the objective basis upon which the whole structure of the faith is constructed. 'If Christ has not risen' says St Paul, 'vain then is our preaching, vain too is your faith. Yes, and we are found false witnesses as to God, in that we have borne witness against God, if the dead do not rise.' (I Cor 15:14–15)"[20]

"Nationalism has been superseded by the doctrine of the Mystical Body, which is as old as Christianity. ... Because Jesus lives in you and me, we are one. ... In the conversion of St Paul, one sentence contains the truth. 'I am Christ whom you persecute.' ... We are one with Christ as Christ is one with the Father. ... That the Mystical Body includes only the Roman Catholic Church is heresy. The Mystical Body is the inseparable oneness of the human race from Adam to the last person. Can I have any animosity toward any Japanese, German, Italian – black or white? If we have animosity, we are liars in Christ."[18]

"The parables of Jesus seek to draw one into the Kingdom, and they challenge us to act and to live from the gift which is experienced therein. But we do not want parables. We want precepts and we want programs. We want good precepts and we want sensible programs. We are frightened by the lonely silences within the parables."[21]

"The cross is not only example and model, but ground, power and norm of the Christian faith."[19]

"For God so loved the world that he gave his only Son, so that everyone who believes in him may not perish but may have eternal life." (Jn 3:16)

For practice

In the coming week, as you go about the business of your days, call to mind from time to time the words of John's Gospel: "God so loved the world … " (John 3:16). Mull over the words. Gently let those words have their way in your mind. Pay attention to the thoughts they engender and feelings they evoke. Listen with the ear of your heart. Be present to the Word who is with you.

4
The Kingdom is within

"The human being is an animal who has the vocation to become God."[22]

Our everyday lives are revealing. People, events and things are evocative. If we are awake to it we will come to know in the depths of our being that life is a mystery to be lived, not a problem to be solved. We will constantly discover that each moment carries the "more than". Life is always summoning us: "Keep listening! Keep searching! Continue the journey! Living is discovering! Life is promise not threat!"

Sacred Scripture offers us a resounding affirmation of this experience. It reveals to us that the Mystery behind the mystery of our days is One who loves us infinitely and unconditionally. Nor does the revelation stop there: the Mystery has been enfleshed in Jesus of Nazareth. Through him, with him and in him we "become participants of the divine nature". (2 Pet 1:4) This is our destiny. We find our human fulfilment in Jesus who is the Christ and this fulfilment is literally divine.

Second-century writer St Irenaeus sums it up nicely: "The Son of God was made human, so that we might become son of God."[23]

Christian reality stands in direct contrast to the Greek mythology of Prometheus. One of his tasks was to steal "fire" from the gods and give it to humankind. The symbol of Pentecost is telling:

> When the day of Pentecost had come, they were all together in one place. And suddenly from heaven there came a sound like the rush of a violent wind, and it filled the entire house where they were sitting. Divided tongues, as of fire, appeared among them, and a tongue rested on each of them. All of them were filled with the Holy Spirit and began to speak in other languages, as the Spirit gave them ability. (Acts 2:1-4)

No such act of "theft" is called for by the God of Abraham, Isaac and Jacob, the God of Jesus Christ and the sender of the Holy Spirit. The "fire" of life – divine life – is given freely. John's Gospel recalls the promise:

> I will not leave you orphaned; I am coming to you. In a little while the world will no longer see me, but you will see me; because I live, you also will live. On that day you will know that I am in my Father, and you in me, and I in you. (Jn 14:18-20)

John's Gospel speaks of this in terms of being "born from above". (See Jn 3:3-8) Paul speaks of it as a "new creation":

> So if anyone is in Christ, there is a new creation: everything old has passed away; see, everything has become new! (2 Cor 5:17. See also Gal 6:15)

This is the work of Baptism. In and through Baptism we become Christians – Christ Persons. It is from this act of "being born from above", becoming a "new creation", that I now derive my identity as a human being, one destined to live the life of God:

> By the grace of baptism "in the name of the Father and of the Son and of the Holy Spirit," we are called to share in the life of the Blessed Trinity, here on earth in the obscurity of faith, and after death in eternal light. (Catechism of the Catholic Church (CCC) 265)

For reflection

Take each text on its own and read it slowly and reflectively. Listen with the ear of the heart. Pause from time to time and listen to any movement within, whether it be a movement of resonance or resistance. Let the process lead you to some kind of words with God.

"The Word became flesh to make us 'partakers of the divine nature' (2 Pet 1:4): 'For this is why the Word became human, and the Son of God became the Son of man: so that we, by entering into communion with the Word and thus receiving divine sonship, might become a son of God' (St Irenaeus, *Against Heresies*, III:19). 'For the Son of God became a human being so that we might become God" (St Athanasius, *On the Incarnation*, 54:3). 'The only-begotten Son of God, wanting to make us sharers in his divinity, assumed our nature, so that he, made human, might make us gods' (St Thomas Aquinas, *Opusculum*, 57:1–4)." (CCC 460)

"The countless lamps which are burning were all lit at the same fire, that is to say they were all lighted and are all shining through the action of one and the same substance. Thus Christians shine brilliantly through the action of the divine fire, the Son of God. Their lamps that have been lit are in the depths of their heart and they shine in his presence during the time they spend on earth, just as he himself shines brilliantly."[24]

"'The kingdom of God is within you' (Lk 17.21). From this we learn that by a heart made pure ... we see in our own beauty the image of the godhead ... You have in you the ability to see God. He who formed you put in your being an immense power. When God created you he enclosed in you the image of his perfection, as the mark of a seal is impressed on wax. But your straying has obscured God's image ... You are like a metal coin: on the whetstone the rust disappears. The coin was dirty, but now it reflects the brightness of the sun and shines in its turn. Like the coin, the inward part of the personality, called the heart by our Master, once rid of the rust that hid its beauty, will rediscover the first likeness and be real ... So when people look at themselves, they will see in themselves the One they are seeking. And this is the joy that will fill their purified hearts. They are looking at their own translucency and finding the model in the image. When the sun is looked at in a mirror, even without any raising of the eyes to heaven, the sun's brightness is seen in the mirror exactly as if the sun's disc itself were being looked at. You cannot contemplate the reality of the light; but if you rediscover the beauty of the image that was put in you at the beginning, you will obtain within yourself the goal of your desires ... The divine image will shine brightly in us in Christ Jesus our Lord, to whom be glory throughout all ages."[25]

For practice

There is a type of question we might call an open question. It does not seek an answer so much as a different way of thinking or a broader perspective or a new attitude to the issue at hand. The response to an open question is to listen – to listen with the ear of the heart. Before an open question we resist the temptation to give an answer. We wait attentively, alert to any movement of thought or feeling. In the coming days use this process to ask the following as open questions: What is happening? What matters? What do you want?

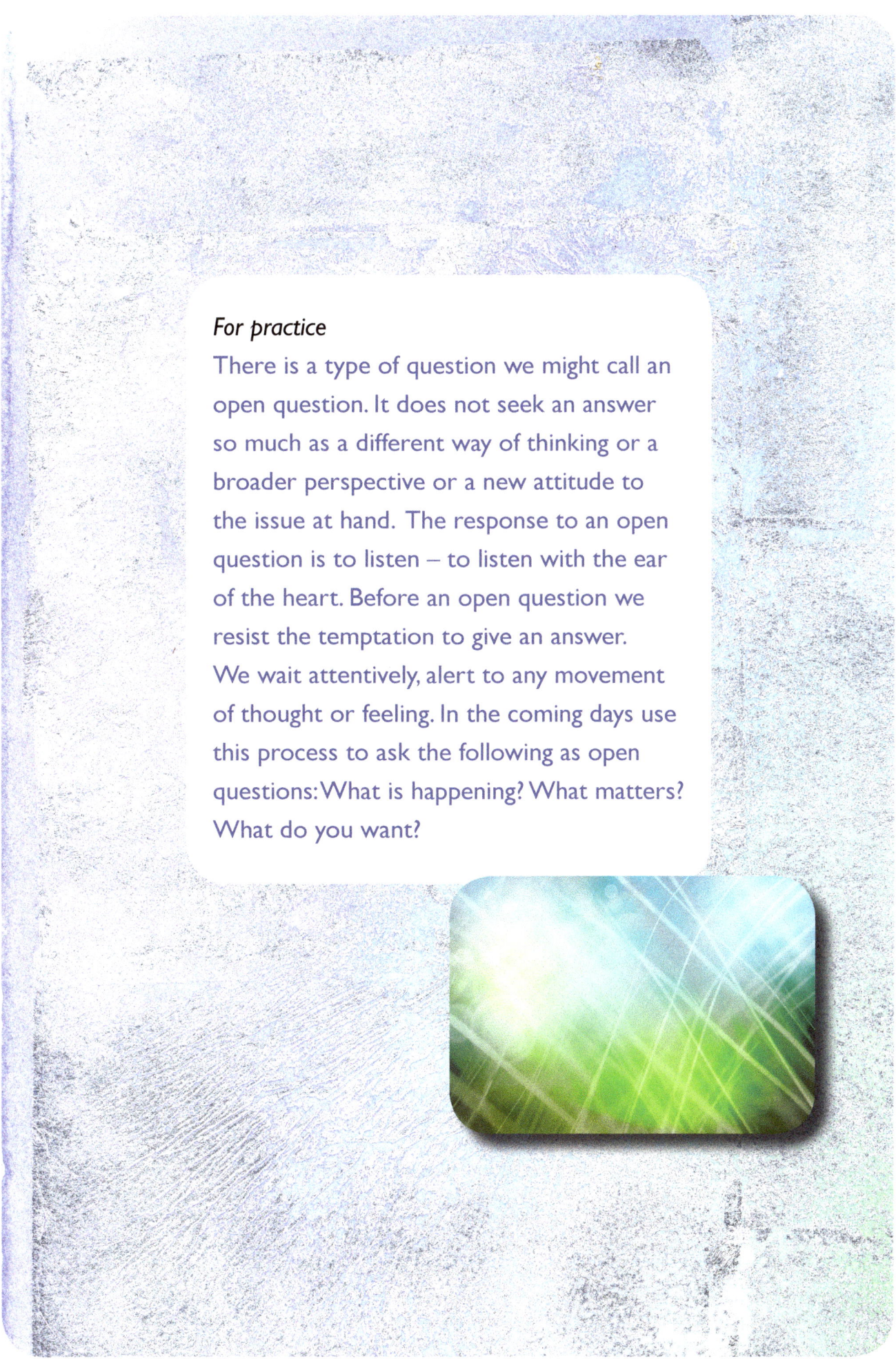

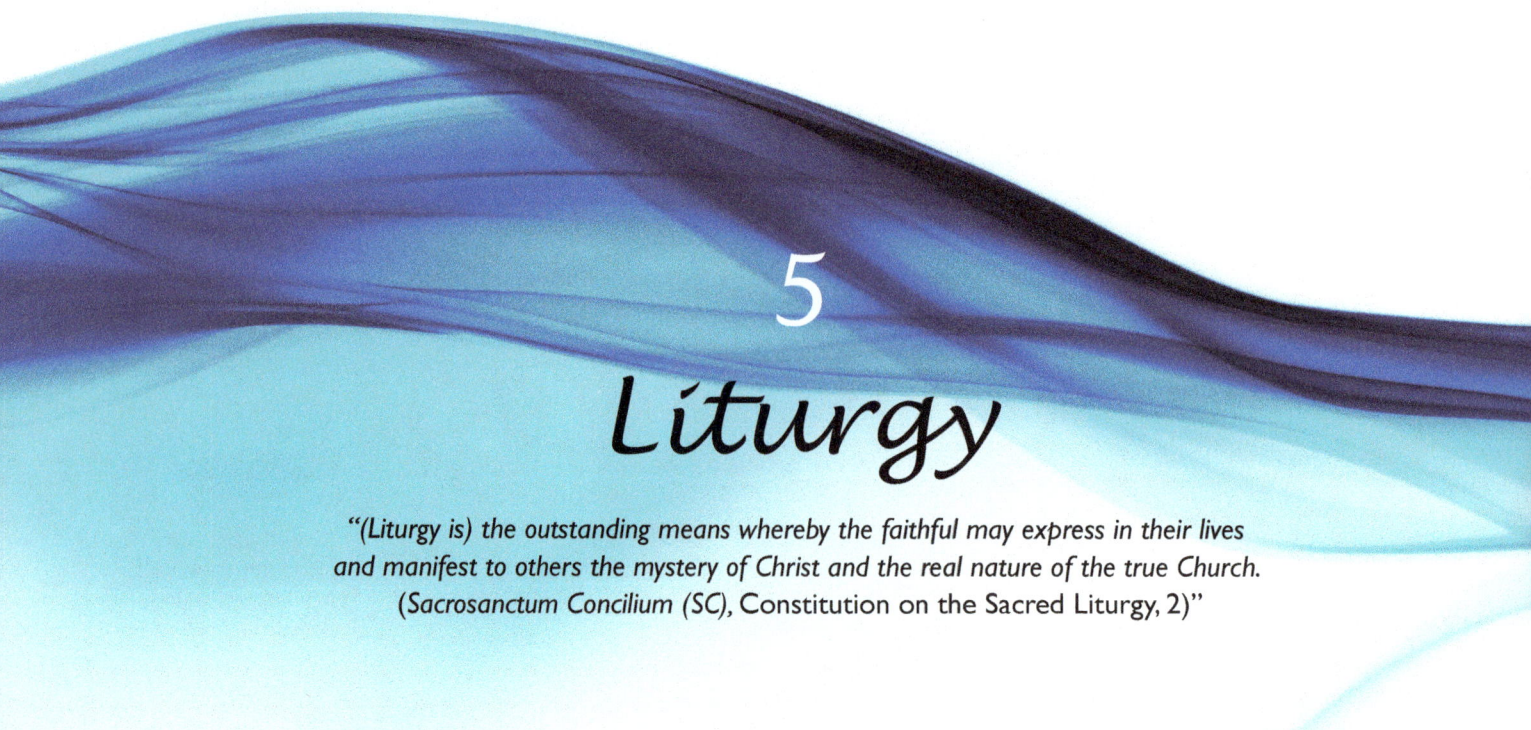

5
Liturgy

"(Liturgy is) the outstanding means whereby the faithful may express in their lives and manifest to others the mystery of Christ and the real nature of the true Church. (Sacrosanctum Concilium (SC), Constitution on the Sacred Liturgy, 2)"

We find our identity as Catholics in the community of the baptised. There is no such thing as a merely private existence. There is no such thing as merely private spirituality, merely private religion or merely private prayer either. Certainly, our life will be personal and in many ways unique, but never merely private. To be human is to be present – to God, self, others and the world. Human existence is, of its nature community-tending.

It is not surprising therefore that the Catholic Tradition gives primary emphasis to the community in prayer. Liturgy is the primary form of prayer in the Catholic Tradition. Liturgy is the public, formal prayer of the Church:

> In the restoration and promotion of the sacred liturgy, the full and active participation by all the people is the aim to be considered before all else; for it is the primary and indispensable source from which the faithful are to derive the true Christian spirit. (*SC* 14)

"The liturgical assembly is first of all a communion in faith."(CCC 1102) This faith is born of the Paschal Mystery. It is nourished and grows by listening to the Word. (CCC 1102) The Word reminds us that God is active in history – our communal as well as our personal histories:

> Christian liturgy not only recalls the events that saved us but actualizes them, makes them present. The Paschal Mystery of Christ is celebrated, not repeated. It is the celebrations that are repeated, and in each celebration there is an outpouring of the Holy Spirit that makes the unique Mystery present. (CCC 1104)

The liturgy is celebrated through the sacraments of Baptism, Eucharist, Confirmation, Marriage, Ordained Ministry, Anointing of the Sick, and Reconciliation, and through the Prayer of the Church – a collection of psalms, readings from sacred Scripture and prayers which are usually prayed in common but may be prayed alone. On those occasions when an individual prays the Prayer of the Church alone, he or she does so in communion with the whole Church and as representing the whole Church.

The Eucharist is the ground and the summit of the whole Christian life in general and the liturgy in particular, "for no Christian community can be built up unless it has its basis and center in the celebration of the most Holy Eucharist."[26] St Paul reminds us that "as often as you eat this bread and drink the cup, you proclaim the Lord's death until he comes". (1 Cor 11:26)

In the celebration of the Eucharist we are at the very centre of God's life and action in the world now. In the Eucharist the Paschal Mystery is quite explicitly invoked and celebrated. This is the most intense form of Christian prayer. All other expressions of Christian prayer must manifest – at least implicitly – the fact that we are a Eucharistic community. Christian prayer flows from the celebration of the Eucharist and leads us back to it.

For reflection

Take each text on its own and read it slowly and reflectively. Listen with the ear of the heart. Pause from time to time and listen to any movement within, whether it be a movement of resonance or resistance. Let the process lead you to some kind of words with God.

"From this it follows that every liturgical celebration, because it is an action of Christ the Priest and of his Body, which is the Church, is a sacred action surpassing all others. No other action of the Church can equal its efficacy by the same title and to the same degree." (SC 7)

"Think of us (Apostles) in this way, as servants of Christ and stewards of God's mysteries." (1 Cor 4:1)

"The liturgy is the summit toward which the activity of the Church is directed; it is also the fount from which all her power flows, for the goal of apostolic endeavour is that all who are made sons of God by faith and baptism should come together to praise God in the midst of his Church, to take part in the Sacrifice and to eat the Lord's Supper." (SC 10)

"If you want to understand the Body of Christ, listen to what the Apostle Paul says to the faithful: 'You are the body of Christ, member for member' (1 Cor 12:27; Rom 12:5). *You* are Christ's own body, his members; thus, *it is your own mystery which is placed on the Lord's table. It is your own mystery that you receive.* For at communion, the priest says, 'The body of Christ,' and you reply 'Amen!' When you say 'Amen,' you are saying yes to what you are. Be a member of Christ's body, then, so that your 'Amen' may be true. For here, we bring nothing of our own. Let us listen to the very same apostle as he speaks about this sacrament: 'Because the loaf of bread is one, we, though many, are one body' (1 Cor 10:17). Understand, and rejoice! Unity, truth, faithfulness, love – all are present. 'One loaf of bread.' What is this one bread? 'We, though many, are one body.' Recall that bread is not made from a single grain, but from many. When you were exorcised, you were ground like wheat. When you were baptized, you were leavened. When you received the fire of the Holy Spirit, you were baked. *Be what you see; receive what you are.*"[27]

For practice

Participate in a liturgy deliberately and reflectively. Be conscious of each movement you and the community make, each ritual that is enacted, each word that is spoken. Be gently but fully present to the Presence in the midst of the faith community – this *human community* – as it celebrates the Mystery of God's love.

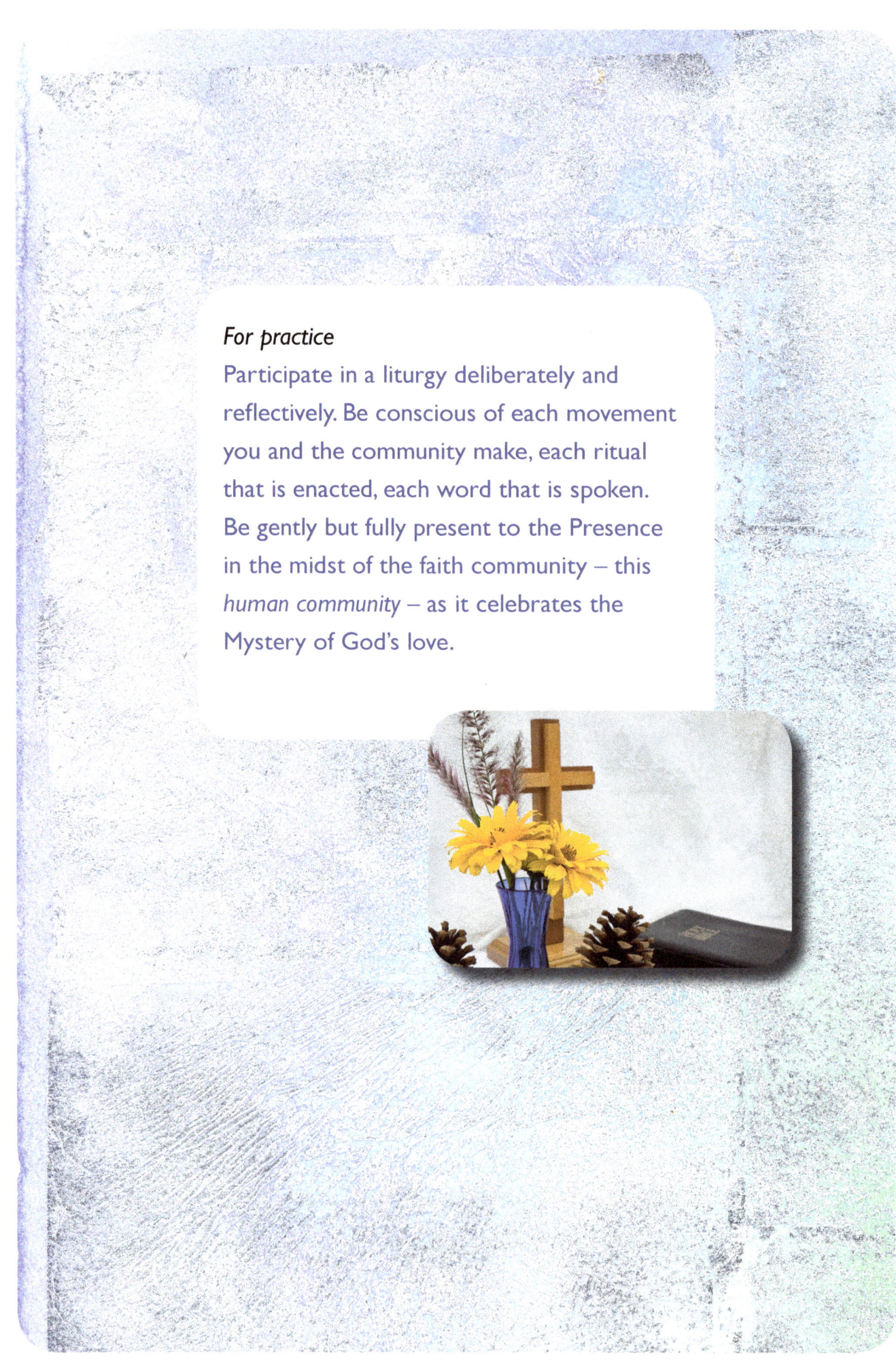

6
The inner journey

"Our real journey in life is interior: it is a matter of growth, deepening, and of an ever greater surrender to the creative action of love and grace in our hearts. Never was it more necessary for us to respond to that action. I pray we may all do so generously."[28]

We are and will ever be a mystery to ourselves. The more we come to know ourselves the more that sense of mystery will grow. Central to this process is an awakening to the world within. That world is not something to be observed with indifference, it summons us on the journey of our lives.

This inner journey is a journey of self-transcendence. The more we come home to ourselves the more we come home to God, other people and the world. In this journey towards our own being we discover the unity of being. It is the very antithesis of egotism and self-absorption.

In reading the Gospels we might overlook the times Jesus seeks solitude. There is, for example, his forty days in the desert (see Mt 4:1–11, Mk 1:12–13 and Lk 3:21–22). But there are many statements in the Gospels that leave us in no doubt that Jesus' journey to Jerusalem was paralleled by a profound inner journey. For example:

> At daybreak he departed and went into a deserted place. (Lk 4:42. See also Mk 1:35)

> When Jesus heard this (i.e. the beheading of John the Baptist), he withdrew from there in a boat to a deserted place by himself. (Mt 14:13. See also Lk 9:18 and Mk 6:31)

Perhaps most telling is the observation by Luke:

> But now more than ever the word about Jesus spread abroad; many crowds would gather to hear him and to be cured of their diseases. But he would withdraw to deserted places and pray. (Lk 5:15-16)

Blaise Pascal (1623–1662) suggests that if we do not embark on this inner journey, our lives cannot be fulfilled:

> I have often said that all men's unhappiness is due to the single fact that they cannot stay quietly in a room.[29]

Sixth-century bishop Dorotheos of Gaza says, suppose we took a compass, put the point in the ground and drew a circle. The bishop then goes on:

> Let us suppose that this circle is the world and that God himself is the centre; the straight lines drawn from the circumference to the centre are the lives of people. To the degree that the saints enter into the things of the spirit, they desire to come near to God; and in proportion to their progress in the things of the spirit, they do in fact come close to God and their neighbour. The closer they are to God the closer they become to one another; and the closer they are to one another, the closer they become to God.[30]

Understanding presence and relationships is the key here. When religion is separated from being present in living relationships – with God, self, others and the world – it will cease to be religion in any true sense of that word and become an ideology. When ideology masquerades as religion and ideologues pretend to be religious, the results will not be good, they may even be quite wicked. Those occasions in history where we find "prayer" accompanying dreadful deeds – as when prayers were said for heretics as they were burned at the stake – can be understood in this way.

For reflection
Take each text on its own and read it slowly and reflectively. Listen with the ear of the heart. Pause from time to time and listen to any movement within, whether it be a movement of resonance or resistance. Let the process lead you to the stillness and quiet deep within. Wait there and listen.

"People who can't stand being alone make the worst company."[31]

"One of the best known of the Desert Fathers of fourth-century Egypt, Saint Serapion the Sidonite, travelled once on pilgrimage to Rome. Here he was told of a celebrated recluse, a woman who lived always in one small room, never going out. Sceptical about her way of life – for he was himself a great wanderer – Serapion called on her and asked: 'Why are you sitting here?' To this she replied: 'I am not sitting, I am on a journey.'"[32]

"When we cry 'Abba! Father', it is the Spirit himself bearing witness with our spirit that we are children of God." (Rom 8:16)

"God, you are my God, I am seeking you, my soul is thirsting for you, my flesh is longing for you, a land parched, weary and waterless; I long to gaze on you in the Sanctuary and to see your power and glory." (Ps 63:1-2)

26 A Friendly Guide to Prayer

For practice

Take time in the coming days to sit still for as long as you can up to twenty minutes. If you find twenty minutes too long, start with say five minutes and extend the time each day. Use a single thought or image or word to still your mind. Listen to what is going on in and around you. Do this several times. On each occasion conclude with a brief conversation with God about what is happening in your life. You might also pray for God's special blessing on someone whom you think might need that blessing.

7
There are many ways

"The Christian faithful have the right to worship God according to the prescriptions of their own rite, approved by the legitimate pastors of the Church, and to follow their own form of spiritual life, consonant with the teaching of the Church."[33]

Jesus is "the Way" (see Jn 14:6) but there are many ways to be in that Way. The Church's Code of Canon Law (1983) acknowledges and confirms this. Each of us is unique. This uniqueness must inevitably be part of our being present to the Presence. If we are faithful to the inner journey described above, we will enter a living paradox: the more we submit to that uniqueness and come home to ourselves, the more we will find ourselves becoming one with God, other people and our world. Uniqueness does not imply disconnection. It does imply being true to ourselves.

The Tradition bears witness to this. Listen, for example, to this story from the Desert Fathers:

> A brother asked one of the elders: "What good thing shall I do and have life thereby?" The old man replied: "God alone knows what is good. However, I have had heard it said that someone inquired of Father Abbot Nisteros the Great, the friend of Abbot Anthony, asking: "What good work shall I do?" and that he replied: "Not all works are alike. For Scripture says that Abraham was hospitable and God was with him; Elias loved solitary prayer and God was with him; and David was humble and God was with him. Therefore, whatever you see your soul desire according to God, do that thing, and you shall keep your heart safe."[34]

The number of those who wrote about prayer and the many ways they approached their subject also testifies to the truth that there are many ways for us to open ourselves to the Presence. We may pray differently and experience prayer differently to the person next to us, but there are some common themes. For example:

Prayerfulness is integral to living.
It can never be regarded as a category on its own, belonging to a separate time and place. Prayerfulness is manifest in the prayerful life, a life open to God, ever-seeking to be at one with God in all things, at all times and in all places. Thus St Paul encouraged the Christians in Thessalonica to pray without ceasing (see 1 Thess 5:17).

Prayerfulness demands a moral commitment.
We cannot realistically expect to become prayerful if we are not embracing our moral responsibilities as followers of the Way. We must face ourselves and hold ourselves open to the primacy of love (see Jn 13:34). Dominican priest Meister Eckhart (1260–1327) puts it concisely when he writes:

> This above all else is needful: you must lay claim to nothing! Let go of yourself and let God act with you and in you as He will. This work is His, this Word is his, this birth is His, in fact every single thing that you are.[35]

In another sermon, Eckhart's gentle words – with just a touch of irony – are full of promise. They remind us that the pursuit of the moral life is in fact the opening of ourselves to the greatest possibilities that can be ours as human beings:

> My dear friend, what harm can it do you to do God the favour of letting Him be God in you?[36]

Prayerfulness includes both process and content. We need to feed our minds and imaginations with good, substantial ideas and images that open us and draw us to the Presence of God – most especially God's presence in Jesus Christ and His Spirit let loose in the world on Calvary. In the monastic tradition there are four different but interlocking practices that keep both process and content happening in a creative tension. The first practice is *slowed down reading*. This is a reflective, ruminating kind of reading sometimes referred to by its Latin name, *lectio divina*. The primary text for *lectio* is the Bible and the primary context is the community. However, other texts and other contexts are not to be excluded. The second practice is *study and research*, sometimes referred to by its Latin name, *meditatio*. The *lectio* will often give rise to questions that need attention. This takes us to other books or knowledgeable people. The third practice is *talking to God*, sometimes referred to as *oratio*. The *lectio* and *meditatio* will often fire the mind and heart, giving rise to informal and spontaneous conversation with God. The fourth practice is *being still and silent in the Presence*, sometimes referred to as *contemplation*. The *lectio*, *meditatio* and *oratio* bring us quite naturally to a moment in which the Psalmist's words become very real: "Be still and know that I am God" (Ps 46:10).

Prayerfulness is a never-ending journey. Our capacity for presence to the Presence can never be exhausted. The more our awareness grows, the more we wake up to what is going on in and around us, the more we will hunger and thirst for the Presence. Again, the Psalmist puts it nicely:

As a deer longs for flowing streams,
so my soul longs for you, O God.
My soul thirsts for God,
for the living God.
(Ps 42:1-2)

For reflection
Take each text on its own and read it slowly and reflectively. Listen with the ear of the heart. Pause from time to time and listen to any movement within, whether it be a movement of resonance or resistance. Let the process lead you to some kind of words with God. If silence beckons, let it be.

"(Prayer) is a desire for God, an indescribable devotion, not of human origin, but a gift of God's grace. ... Once (you) have tasted this food, (you) are set alight by an eternal desire for the Lord, the fiercest of fires lighting up (your) soul."[37]

"Be still before the LORD, and wait patiently for him." (Ps 37:7)

"Humble yourselves therefore under the mighty hand of God, so that he may exalt you in due time. Cast all your anxiety on him, because he cares for you. Discipline yourselves, keep alert. Like a roaring lion your adversary the devil prowls around, looking for someone to devour. Resist him, steadfast in your faith, for you know that your brothers and sisters in all the world are undergoing the same kinds of suffering. And after you have suffered for a little while, the God of all grace, who has called you to his eternal glory in Christ, will himself restore, support, strengthen, and establish you. To him be the power forever and ever. Amen.
(1 Pet 5:6-11)

"I was in an underground train, a crowded train in which all sorts of people jostled together, sitting and strap-hanging workers of every description going home at the end of the day. Quite suddenly I saw with my mind, but as vividly as a wonderful picture, Christ in them all. But I saw more than that; not only was Christ in every one of them, living in them, dying in them, rejoicing in them, sorrowing in them – but because He was in them, and because they were here the whole world was here too, here in this underground train; not only the world as it was at that moment, not only all the people in all the countries of the world, but all those people who had lived in the past, and all those yet to come. I came out into the street, and walked for a long time in the crowds. It was the same here, on every side, in every passer-by, everywhere – Christ."[38]

For practice

In the Jewish tradition there is the practice of "blessing" God. There are "blessings" for bread or vegetables, for lightning or a rainbow, for recovering from an illness or for the clothes that one wears, for freedom, for waking up and so on. In our Eucharist we say such "blessing" prayers at the Offertory – "Blessed are you Lord God of all creation ... ". As you go about the business of your life in the coming days, "bless" God for whatever comes to your mind.

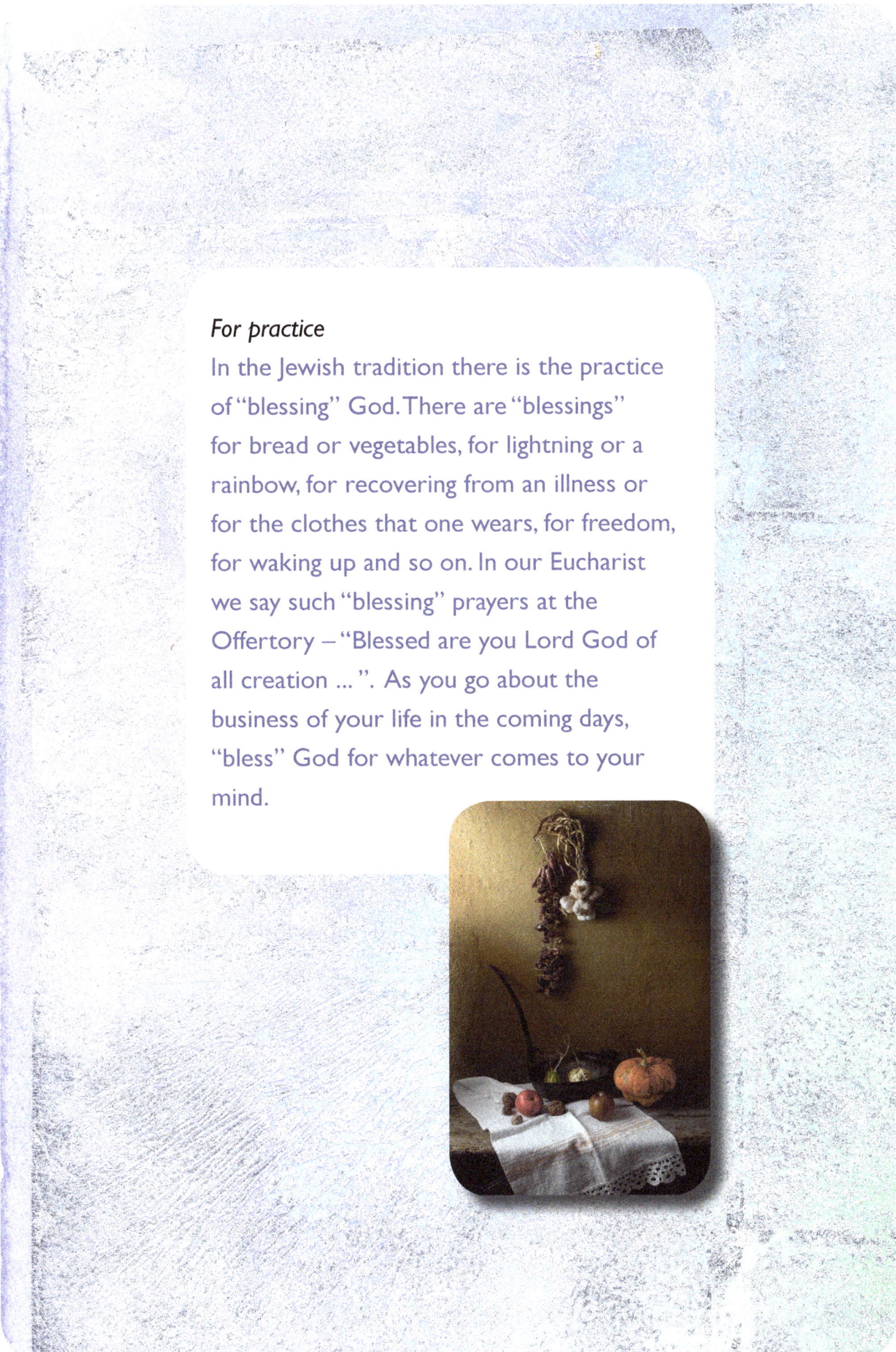

8
The body

*"People who are carnal are not more capable of acting spiritually,
nor spiritual people of acting carnally, than deeds of unbelief are possible to the faithful,
or deeds of faith to the unbelieving. But with you, even what you do in the flesh is spiritual,
for your actions are all done in Jesus Christ."*[39]

It seems to be a very human tendency – not just of religious folk – to disengage or disconnect from the body. Ironically, this can take the form of using the body, as if it was some kind of a plaything or instrument or mere object. This disengagement and disconnection can also be seen in the obesity epidemic that afflicts our society, in various eating disorders and in addictions such as smoking, excessive use of alcohol and drugs, and the pre-occupation with sex.

The religious sphere – specifically the Christian life – has its own particular manifestations of this disengagement from the body. For example, St Jerome (331–420) wrote:

> While the Apostles yet remained upon the earth, while the blood of Jesus was almost smoking upon the soil of Judaea, some asserted that the body of the Lord was a phantom.[40]

From the very earliest days, the heresy known as Docetism was evident in Christianity. St Ignatius of Antioch alludes to it in his Letter to the Ephesians. More broadly it lingers in the Catholic Tradition variously as an overly pious or saccharine approach to the Christian life often accompanied by a more or less strong distrust of the body.

This is not the place to explore what it is that so frequently has us in conflict with our bodily being, whether we are religious or not. However, it is the place to raise the issue, because the body is an integral part of becoming a human being and therefore an integral part of becoming a *prayerful* person. We need to be aware of the dangers in order to avoid the pitfalls and to maximise the benefits. Yes, we are a "new creation" through our being baptised into Christ (see 2 Cor 5:17 and Gal 6:15). This "new creation" is an affair of the whole person, including the body, not just the spirit.

Asceticism, which comes from the Greek word *Askesis*, meaning "exercise" or "training", is a

> The English word Docetism comes from the Greek word *Dokein*, meaning "to seem" or "to appear". Docetism is therefore the false belief that Jesus only appeared to be in the flesh. By extension, this false belief manifests itself more generally in a tendency to denigrate or even deny the bodily dimension of the Christian life.
>
> St Ignatius was Bishop of Antioch when he was arrested and taken to Rome where he was martyred in the Coliseum about the year 110. On his way to Rome, he wrote to the various churches in Asia Minor. We have those letters and they provide us with a rich insight into both Ignatius and the life of the Church at that time.

32 A Friendly Guide to Prayer

crucial part of the Catholic Tradition for this very reason. It serves a twofold purpose: knowledge and freedom. By certain practices – such as fasting and deliberately doing without certain things – we train our bodily selves so that we come to know experientially and, as it were, instinctively what matters and what is good for us. We also grow in the freedom to choose what matters and what is good for us.

Here again the Tradition is very aware of the potential for missing the mark:

> Abba Antony said: "Some wear down their bodies by fasting. But because they have no discretion, it puts them further from God."[41]

Consider the bodily expressions evident in Catholic liturgy. We enter the church, dip a hand into Holy Water and make the sign of the Cross, we genuflect or bow, we kneel or sit or stand, and we process to the altar to hold out our hands to receive the Bread of Life – "Take, eat; this is my body" (Mt 26:26). We light charcoal and sprinkle it with incense and the aroma draws us into the ritual through our bodily capacity to smell. We reach out our hands and greet each other with a sign of peace. We anoint with oil, light candles, pour water over the forehead – occasionally we fully immerse people – and we clothe the body with special garments and robes. We sing, speak or remain silent. Everywhere there are statues, paintings and symbols to catch the eye and remind us of who we are, where we are and what is happening. Liturgy is a very bodily event.

In some cultures, song and dance, for example, are important bodily expressions. Song and dance can tell stories, celebrate and express what speech can never say. Similarly, certain body postures and breathing practices are used to bring about stillness and focus the mind. Any of these may be a legitimate and valuable means to promote prayerfulness.

Routine, regularity and constancy can achieve the ascetical ends of knowledge and freedom mentioned above. They are not ends in themselves but means. For example, physical stillness, sitting in a certain way, standing, walking, dancing or even lying down can set us free from bodily tensions and distractions of the mind so we are more able be present to the Presence.

In the Prologue to John's Gospel we read: "the Word became flesh and lived among us". (Jn 1:14) There is no such thing as "the spiritual life" that is not at once also "the bodily life". The two are dimensions of the one. We could take the central truth of God's Incarnation – the enfleshing of God – as the central truth of our daily lives. It is best understood as a verb rather than a noun. As people baptised into Christ (see Rom 6:3) our lives are a participation in the Incarnation which goes on happening. The enfleshing of God is happening in each of us daily. Our bodily existence is an instrument of the fulfilment of God's promise to be with us:

> Your body is a temple of the Holy Spirit within you, which you have from God, and you are not your own. For you were bought with a price; therefore glorify God in your body. (1 Cor 6:19-20)

The body

For reflection

Take each text on its own and read it slowly and reflectively. Listen with the ear of the heart. Pause from time to time and listen to any movement within, whether it be a movement of resonance or resistance. Let the process lead you to some kind of words with God.

"Do you not know that your body is a temple of the Holy Spirit within you, which you have from God, and that you are not your own? For you were bought with a price; therefore glorify God in your body. (1 Cor 6:19-20)

"Once Abbot Anthony was conversing with some brethren, and a hunter who was after game in the wilderness came upon them. He saw Abbot Anthony and the brothers enjoying themselves, and disapproved. Abbot Anthony said: Put an arrow in your bow and shoot it. This he did. Now shoot another, said the elder. And another, and another. The hunter said: If I bend my bow all the time it will break. Abbot Anthony replied: So it is also in the work of God. If we push ourselves beyond measure, the brethren will soon collapse. It is right therefore from time to time to relax their efforts."[42]

"When you have eaten your fill and have built fine houses and live in them, and when your herds and flocks have multiplied, and your silver and gold is multiplied, and all that you have is multiplied, then do not exalt yourself, forgetting the Lord your God, who brought you out of the land of Egypt, out of the house of slavery, who led you through the great and terrible wilderness, an arid wasteland with poisonous snakes and scorpions. He made water flow for you from flint rock, and fed you in the wilderness with manna that your ancestors did not know, to humble you and to test you, and in the end to do you good. Do not say to yourself, 'My power and the might of my own hand have gotten me this wealth.' But remember the LORD your God, for it is he who gives you power to get wealth, so that he may confirm his covenant that he swore to your ancestors, as he is doing today." (Deut 8:12-18)

"Now the nature of our body was created, not by an evil principle, as the Manicheans pretend, but by God. Hence we can use it for God's service, according to Romans 6:13 – "Present your members as instruments for justice unto God." Consequently, out of the love of charity with which we love God, we ought to love our bodies also."[43]

For practice

Several times in the coming days prepare your food – whether it is a cup of coffee or a full meal – in a slow and reflective way. Become aware of what is happening, both within you and in the actions you are doing.

Go to a liturgy and be mindful of what is happening – gestures, postures, smells, sounds, sights. Ask some open questions, like: Why are they happening? What are you feeling in your belly? Listen within.

9
The mind

"God is wisdom and He wills to be loved not only sweetly but wisely; as St Paul says: 'Let your service be one that is worthy of thinking beings' (Rom 12:1). For if you neglect knowledge, the spirit of error will lead you astray effortlessly by means of your own zeal. The cunning enemy has no more effective strategy for robbing the heart of love than to induce a person to indulge it rashly and unreasonably."[44]

We find a basic principle at work in human growth: living is moving. We are all pilgrims, always moving on, never quite arriving. Every hello contains a goodbye, every dawn a dusk, every arrival a departure. The "more than", present in every moment, summons us. It is as if each person, event and thing is saying, "Not me, more than me. Not this, more than this."

Facing and submitting to the truth of things leads us beyond things to no-thing. Authentic speech emerges from silence and returns us to silence. Images lead us beyond images, ideas leads us beyond ideas. Our bodily being will take us beyond body. Our knowing develops, grows and deepens into a profound not-knowing – a knowing that is beyond words. St Paul shines the light of faith beautifully on this vision of the human journey:

> For now we see in a mirror, dimly, but then we will see face to face. Now I know only in part; then I will know fully, even as I have been fully known. And now faith, hope, and love abide, these three; and the greatest of these is love. (1 Cor 13:12-13)

It is essential that we employ the mind in the business of developing a prayerful life. For example, in the Eucharistic liturgy every Sunday we say the Nicene Creed. This is a statement of the central truths of our faith. The prayerful life assumes some knowledge of those truths – the deeper the better. If we do not employ the mind well, giving it something to focus on, it will tend to become a source of distraction, leading us away from being present to the Presence.

In the Catholic Tradition there is a form of prayer generally referred to as discursive meditation. We find it, for example, in the first week of St Ignatius of Loyola's *Spiritual Exercises*. It is also well described in St Francis de Sales' *Introduction to the Devout Life*, chapters 9–18. Discursive meditation was the kind of practice generally encouraged in the medieval monasteries in conjunction with *lectio divina*. (See Chapter 7)

> ST IGNATIUS OF LOYOLA was born in Loyola, Spain about 1491 and died in Rome in 1556. St Ignatius was a soldier as a young man. He underwent a profound conversion during a time of convalescence then founded the Society of Jesus (Jesuits). His *Spiritual Exercises* is a masterpiece of guidance from the early stages of prayer to contemplation.

In the practice of discursive meditation, we are encouraged, for example, to think carefully about certain truths of the faith, and events and teachings in the life of Jesus. This intellectual work, done in faith, leads us towards at least two outcomes. Firstly, the truths we reflect on sink deeply into our consciousness and find a home there, thus shaping our lives. Secondly, the process of thinking about God's revelation leads us quite naturally towards a conversation with God.

Thinking rationally, however, about this or that truth is actually superficial compared to the knowledge of faith. Rational reflection represents the beginnings of a journey. Faith transforms the human mind and ultimately the human person. St Paul says, "we are those who have the mind of Christ". (1 Cor 2:16. See also Phil 2:5: "Make your own the mind of Christ Jesus.") St Clement of Rome writes:

> Through Him we can look up to the highest heaven and see, as in a glass, the peerless perfection of the face of God. Through Him the eyes of our heart are opened, and our dim and clouded understanding unfolds like a flower to the light; for through Him the Lord permits us to taste the wisdom of eternity.[45]

> ST CLEMENT is generally reckoned to be the third successor to St Peter as the leader of the Church in Rome. He is best known for the Letter he sent to the Christians in Corinth.

The transformation to this depth of thinking is experienced as a journey through *not knowing*. The rational mind can grasp only so much. If the greater depths of the human mind are to be opened up, it must be stripped and purged so that it can move beyond merely rational knowing. The rational mind must come to the humbling experience of its limits if it is to grow towards its wonderful possibilities in Christ.

There is a classic text that deals with this experience. It is by an unknown English author of the fourteenth century and is called *The Cloud of Unknowing*:

> Lift up your heart to God with a humble impulse of love; and have himself as your aim, not any of his goods. Take care that you avoid thinking of anything but himself, so that there is nothing for your reason or your will to work on, except himself. Do all that in you lies to forget all the creatures that God ever made, and their works, so that neither your thought nor your desire be extended to any of them, neither in general nor in particular. Let them alone and pay no attention to them … it is the easiest exercise of all and most readily accomplished when a soul is helped by grace in this felt desire; otherwise it would be extraordinarily difficult for you to make this exercise. Do not hang back then, but labour in it until you experience the desire. For when you first begin to undertake it, all that you find is a darkness, a sort of cloud of unknowing; you cannot tell what it is, except that you experience in your will a simple reaching out to God. The darkness and cloud is always between you and your God, no matter what you do, and it prevents you from seeing him clearly by the light of understanding in your reason, and from experiencing him in sweetness of love in your affection. So set yourself to rest in this darkness as long as you can, always crying out after him whom you love. For if you are to experience him or to see him at all, in so far as it is possible here, it must always be in this cloud and in this darkness. So if you labour at it with all your attention as I bid you, I trust, in his mercy, that you will reach this point.[46]

St John of the Cross makes it clear that discursive meditation is a beginning form of prayer and individuals may move beyond it "after a very short time".[47] John has some strong words to say about those spiritual directors who do not recognise this movement and encourage the individual to persist in discursive meditation.[48] That movement beyond discursive meditation is towards greater depth and simplicity. It is also a movement through lesser delights and satisfactions towards the greatest delight and satisfaction. Hence, we must pass through "dark nights" of the sense and the spirit. The greatest delight is found in the fulfilment of the soul's deepest longing:

> The soul's center is God. When it has reached God with all the capacity of its being and the strength of its operation and inclination, it will have attained its final and deepest center in God, it will know, love, and enjoy God with all its might. … It is noteworthy, then, that love is the soul's inclination, strength and power in making its way to God, for love unites it with God.[49]

> ST JOHN OF THE CROSS was born near Avila, Spain in 1542 and died at Ubeda, Spain, in 1591. He aided St Teresa of Avila in founding the Discalced Carmelites. His poetry and prose descriptions are among the finest works on the spiritual depths of the human journey.

For reflection
Take each text on its own and read it slowly and reflectively. Listen with the ear of the heart. Pause from time to time and listen to any movement within, whether it be a movement of resonance or resistance. You may be led to speak a word of praise or simply look towards God with praise in your heart.

"Indeed it is better to keep quiet and be, than to make fluent professions and not be. No doubt it is fine to instruct others, but only if the speaker practises what he preaches. One such Teacher there is: *He who spake the word and it was done* (Ps 33:9); and what he achieved even by his silences was well worthy of the Father. A man who has truly mastered the utterances of Jesus will also be able to apprehend his silence, and thus reach full spiritual maturity, so that his own words have the force of actions and his silences the significance of speech."[50]

"O Lord, you have searched me and known me.
You know when I sit down and when I rise up;
you discern my thoughts from far away.
You search out my path and my lying down, and are acquainted with all my ways. Even before a word is on my tongue,
O Lord, you know it completely.
You hem me in, behind and before,
and lay your hand upon me.
Such knowledge is too wonderful for me;
it is so high that I cannot attain it."
(Ps 139:1-6)

"Truth needs to be sought, found and expressed within the 'economy' of charity, but charity in its turn needs to be understood, confirmed and practised in the light of truth. In this way, not only do we do a service to charity enlightened by truth, but we also help give credibility to truth, demonstrating its persuasive and authenticating power in the practical setting of social living. This is a matter of no small account today, in a social and cultural context which relativizes truth, often paying little heed to it and showing increasing reluctance to acknowledge its existence."[51]

"I know my own and my own know me, just as the Father knows me and I know the Father." (Jn 10:14-15)

For practice

Read the Gospel story of Jesus' disciples picking corn on the Sabbath in Matthew 12:1–8 or Luke 6:1–5. Reflect on that story, using questions like: What is the significance of the Sabbath in the Jewish tradition? How does Jesus regard the Sabbath? What might be going on between the religious authorities and Jesus? Is there any Sabbath in your life? Think of other questions to gently promote prayerful reflection. Quietly pause from time to time and stay with a particular thought. If you have access to other material on this Scripture passage, take some time to read that. Speak with Jesus about the thoughts that arise from this reflection. Acknowledge frankly any questions you have. Conclude with some kind of personal prayer.

10
The imagination

" … imagination has the means, which pure intellect has not, of stimulating those powers of the mind from which action proceeds."[52]

John Henry Cardinal Newman represents the best of the tradition in his emphasis on imagination in the spiritual life.[53] Imagination gives energy and impetus in a way that abstract ideas cannot. This is manifest in a typical Catholic church. The architecture is full of symbols, there are generally statues of saints, paintings and frescoes. The great cathedrals of Europe are particularly fine examples of this. The appeal is to the imagination.

> **JOHN HENRY NEWMAN** was born in London in 1801 and died in Birmingham in 1890. He converted from High Anglicanism to Roman Catholicism in 1845. Newman was a brilliant thinker and writer.

Imagination is essential to our remaining connected with reality. Imagination is also essential to our receiving the story of God's love into our lives. This story cannot be appropriated and lived through syllogisms and abstract propositions. The primary instruments of this story of God's love must be lived examples, parables, symbols, rituals, various art forms and images that appeal to our imaginations and thus open us towards ultimate reality.

One of the classics of the Catholic Tradition on prayer is *The Interior Castle*, written by St Teresa of Avila. In this work St Teresa develops the image of a castle with seven "mansions" or "dwelling places". When describing the fifth mansion, she illustrates our life in Christ with a lengthy description of the life cycle of a silk worm. This is a work of imagination that communicates immense wisdom.[54]

> **ST TERESA OF AVILA** was born in Avila, Spain in 1515 and died in Alba de Tormes, Spain in 1582. She is the founder of the Discalced Carmelites, and one of the greatest guides in the spiritual life. She is a Doctor of the Church.

In the previous chapter we spoke of discursive meditation, noting its dependence on mind. Actually, imagination is also part of that process. Near the beginning of *Spiritual Exercises*, St Ignatius instructs the one doing the exercises as follows:

> Here it is to be noted that, in a visible contemplation or meditation – as, for instance, when one contemplates Christ our Lord, Who is visible – the composition will be to see with the sight of the imagination the corporeal place where the thing is found which I want to contemplate … as, for instance, a Temple or Mountain …[55]

The imagination is used to construct a scene – normally from the Gospels – which will then aid thoughtful reflection on the life and teaching of Jesus and its implications for us. Unfortunately, for a number of historical reasons, abstract thought has tended to dominate thinking in recent centuries. However, since the Second Vatican Council there has been a growing appreciation of the Catholic Tradition and a rediscovery of the place of imagination.

St Augustine honours imagination beautifully – and in so doing also honours all forms of artistic expression – when he says: "God is ineffable. So, as you can't speak and don't have the right to keep silent either, what is left for you but to sing?"[56]

For reflection
Take each text on its own and read it slowly and reflectively. Listen with the ear of the heart. Pause from time to time and listen to any movement within, whether it be a movement of resonance or resistance. Can you relate this to your life?

"When you visualized a man or woman carefully, you could always begin to feel pity – that was a quality God's image carried with it. When you saw the lines at the corners of the eyes, the shape of the mouth, how the hair grew, it was impossible to hate. Hate was just a failure of imagination."[57]

"The most significant result of the debate (on the Church, in the First Session of the Second Vatican Council) was the profound realization that the Church has been described, in its two thousand years, not so much by verbal definitions as in the light of images. Most of the images are, of course, strictly biblical. The theological value of the images has been stoutly affirmed by the Council. The notion that you must begin with an Aristotelian definition was simply bypassed. In its place, a biblical analysis of the significance of the images was proposed."[58]

"When I look at your heavens,
the work of your fingers,
the moon and the stars that
you have established;
what are human beings that
you are mindful of them,
mortals that you care for them?
Yet you have made them
a little lower than God,
and crowned them with glory and honor.
You have given them dominion
over the works of your hands;
you have put all things under their feet,
all sheep and oxen,
and also the beasts of the field,
the birds of the air, and the fish of the sea,
whatever passes along the paths of the seas.
O LORD, our Sovereign,
how majestic is your name
in all the earth!" (Ps 8:3-9)

"The kingdom of heaven is like treasure hidden in a field, which someone found and hid; then in his joy he goes and sells all that he has and buys that field." (Mt 13:44)

The imagination 41

For practice

Read the Healing of the Blind Man, Bartimaeus, in Mark 10:46–52. Let the scene come alive for you. See who is there, what they are doing, the landscape. Then let your attention rest on Jesus. Listen within as you see him there. Watch the action of the story. Hear the words. Then imagine Jesus looks directly at you. Let come what will come. If you are led to speak, then speak. If you are led to silence, then remain silent.

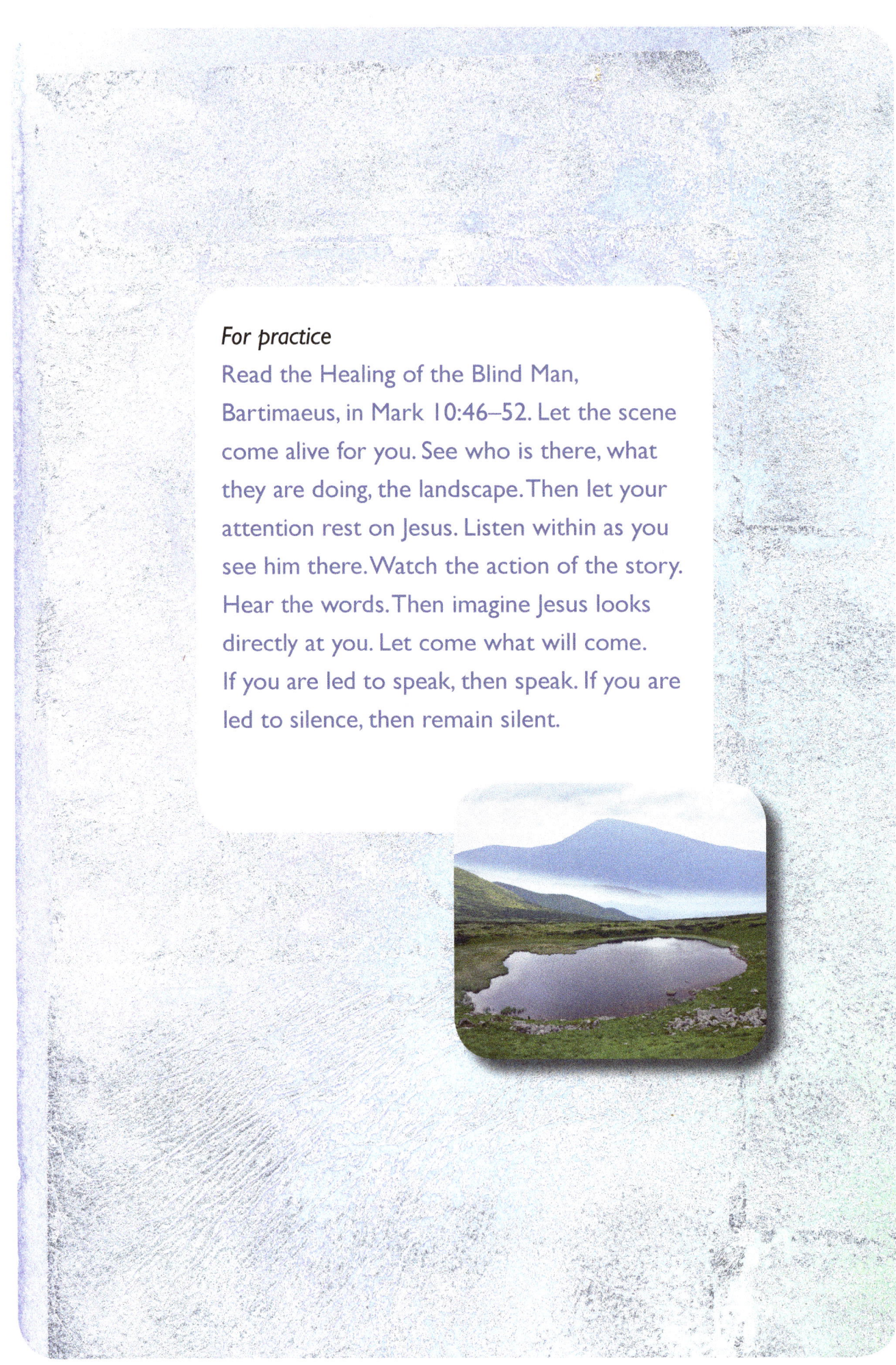

11
The emotions

"Consider how great is the grace of intimacy which results from the encounter of the soul with the Word, and how great the confidence which follows this intimacy! I think such a soul need not fear to say, 'My beloved is mine;' for she perceives that she loves, and loves ardently, and has no doubt that she is loved ardently in return. ... she knows that the initiative lies with the Bridegroom. She knows then without any doubt, ... that she who loves is herself loved. And so it is: the love of God gives birth to the love of the soul for God, his surpassing affection fills the soul with affection, and his concern evokes concern."[59]

In this passage from one of St Bernard's remarkable Sermons on the Song of Songs, we find deep insights that are both psychological and theological. St Bernard recognises that we are creatures, made in the image and likeness of God who is love. There is, therefore, in our very makeup as human beings, something of this capacity for infinite love. We long to be in love – literally to *be* in love. Love is our origin and our destiny. When we immerse ourselves in the sacred Scriptures and the liturgy, when we give ourselves daily to listening with the ear of the heart to what is happening, we actually begin to feel that we are loved by God. The *notion* that we are loved infinitely and unconditionally becomes the *experience* of being loved infinitely and unconditionally. This is pure gift. It is also the true ground of prayerfulness and the prayerful life.

Implicit in St Bernard's statement is a fundamental issue of right order. Disconnected or disassociated from God, emotions will tend to be more or less destructive, being centred on self rather than God. St Augustine sums this up nicely:

> (Those) who live according to God in the pilgrimage of this life, both fear and desire, and grieve and rejoice. And because their love is rightly placed, all these affections of theirs are right.[60]

So the challenge is not to rid ourselves of emotion or suppress emotion or in any way live as if emotion is unimportant. The issue is one of grounding. All our human faculties, including our emotions, when grounded in the experience of knowing in our bones that we are loved infinitely and unconditionally, will tend towards their right end.

This in turn points us towards two experiences which ground our lives. The first is *compunction* and the second is *discernment*.

Compunction is a multi-layered experience in which we simultaneously come to two distinct but inseparable realisations. At one and the same time we realise the truth of our deep need of God's liberating love and the truth of the Presence of that liberating love. The first realisation brings with it such feelings as sorrow, remorse, sadness and perhaps fear. The second realisation brings with it such feelings as relief, release, joy, peace and confidence in God's Presence. Compunction – from the Latin word *pungere*, meaning "to pierce" – will often enough be accompanied by the gift of tears.

Compunction comes, not as conquest but as gift. We make ourselves available for that gift by our honesty, our generous efforts to live a good life, our immersion in the sacred Scriptures and the liturgy, and constant listening with the ear of the heart. Compunction is an experience of more or less deep conversion.

Discernment, as taught by St Ignatius of Loyola, also serves to heighten our experience of emotion in the service of our relationship with God. St Ignatius says right at the outset: "It is not knowing much, but realising and relishing things interiorly, that contents and satisfies the soul."[61] This involves a movement through "consolations" and "desolations".

In discerning these experiences, we are looking more to the cause than the intent. Thus discernment endeavours to address the question: where does this experience of "consolation" or "desolation" come from?

Those emotions – and related urges, desires, inclinations and so on – that have us moving towards the good are assumed by us to come from a good source or "spirit". Those that have us moving towards that which is not good are assumed by us to come from an evil source or "spirit". Typically, when we are moving towards the good we experience a certain "consolation", when moving towards evil, we experience a certain "desolation". It can take great wisdom at times to discern the difference.

Finally, the best of the Tradition is at one in saying that emotion is not to be sought or clung to or interpreted simplistically. For example, St Ignatius points out that one reason for "desolation" is to help us realise that "all is the gift and grace of God our Lord, and that we may not build a nest in a thing that is not ours".[62] St John of the Cross observes:

> It must be understood that if a person experiences some grand spiritual communication or feeling or knowledge, he should not think that his experiences are similar to the clear and essential vision of possession of God, or that the communication, no matter how remarkable it is, signifies a more notable possession of God or union with Him. It should be known too that if all these sensible and spiritual communications are wanting and a person lives in dryness, darkness, and dereliction, he must not think that God is any more absent than in the former case. A person, actually, cannot have certain knowledge from the one state that he is in God's grace, nor from the other that he is not.[63]

> "Can a woman forget her nursing child,
> or show no compassion for
> the child of her womb?
> Even these may forget,
> yet I will not forget you." (Isa 49:15)

For reflection

Take each text on its own and read it slowly and reflectively. Listen with the ear of the heart. Pause from time to time and listen to any movement within, whether it be a movement of resonance or resistance. Let the process lead you to some kind of words with God.

"He who has a heartfelt love for God is known by him. For people grow in the love of God in the measure in which they take that love into their inmost soul. Which is why, afterwards, such people passionately long for the illumination of knowledge to the point of feeling it in their very bones, no longer aware of themselves but wholly transformed by the love of God. Such people are in this life without being in it. They still live in their own bodies but unceasingly go out to God through love by the very momentum of their soul. Henceforward, their hearts burning with the fire of love they adhere to God with a sort of irresistible desire, as if quite torn away from the love of self by the love of God."[64]

"This *state of prayer* within us is something we always carry about, like a hidden treasure of which we are not consciously aware – or hardly so. Somewhere our heart is going full pelt, but we do not feel it. We are deaf to our praying heart, love's savour escapes us, we fail to see the light in which we live. For our heart, our true heart, is asleep; and it has to be woken up, gradually – through the course of a whole lifetime. So it is not really hard to pray. It was given us long since. But very seldom are we conscious of our own prayer. Every technique of prayer is attuned to that purpose. We have to become conscious of what we have already received, must learn to feel, to distinguish it in the full and peaceful assurance of the Spirit, this prayer rooted and operative somewhere deep inside us. It must be brought to the surface of our consciousness. Little by little it will saturate and captivate our faculties, mind and soul and body. Our psyche and even our body must learn to answer to the rhythm of this prayer, be stirred to prayer from within, be incited to prayer, as dry wood is set ablaze. One of the Fathers puts it tersely as this: 'The monk's ascesis: to set wood ablaze.' Prayer then, is nothing other than that unconscious *state of prayer* which in the course of time has become completely conscious. Prayer is the *abundantia cordis*, the abundance of the heart, as the saying goes in the Gospels: 'For a person's words flow out of what fills the heart' (Mt 12:34, Lk 6:45). Prayer is a heart that overflows with joy, thanksgiving, gratitude and praise. It is the *abundance* of a heart that is truly awake."[65]

The imagination

For practice

Read the post-Resurrection account of Jesus asking Peter three times, "Do you love me?" (see Jn 21:15–19). Think of the context. Imagine who is there and what they are doing. How do you think Peter feels? What is your gut reaction?

In the coming days, pause and ask yourself the open question from time to time: what am I feeling?

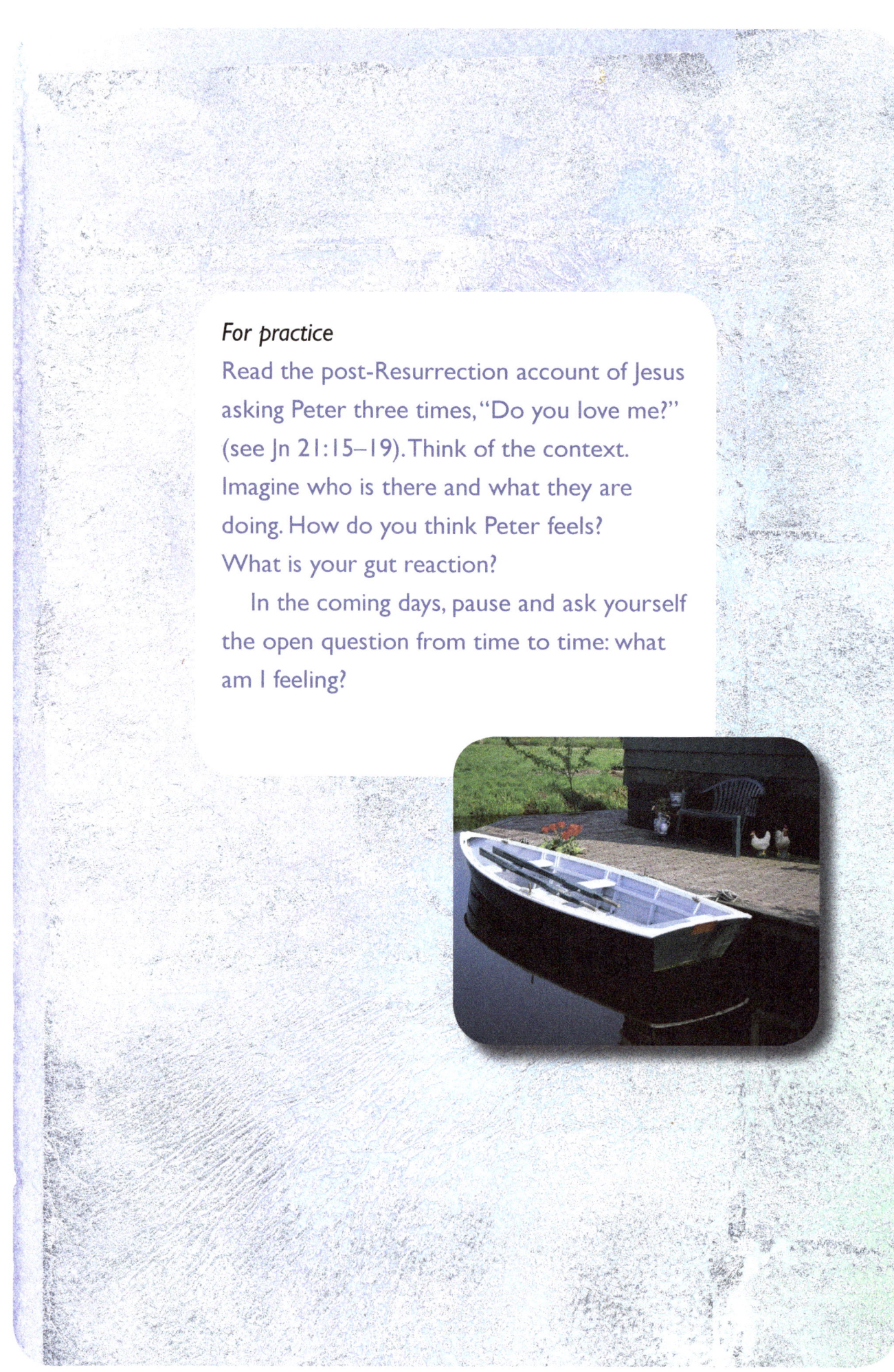

12
Simplicity

*"There is no need to lose oneself in speaking.
It is enough to hold out one's hands and say: Lord, as you know and will, have mercy.
If the combat presses hard, say: To the rescue!
God knows what is needful for you and will have pity on you."*[66]

In the first millennium, there is very little instruction on *how* to pray. It was clearly thought to be a straightforward matter. Macarius became renowned for the simple method of prayer which became known in Greek as *monologistos* – that is "one word" – prayer. The prayer was usually not literally "one word" but a very simple statement that expressed the depths both of the human heart and the Gospel.

Various formulae were suggested, generally with a particular focus on the name of Jesus. Thus we find the same Macarius suggesting:

> Be attentive to this name of Our Lord, Jesus Christ, in contrition of heart; when your lips are moving draw it to yourself and do not lead it into your mind only to repeat it, but think of your invocation: "Our Lord Jesus, the Christ, have mercy on me," then, in repose you will see His divinity reposing on you. It will drive away the darkness of the passions that are within you, it will purify the interior man with the purification of Adam when he was in paradise – this blessed name that John the Evangelist called on, saying: "light of the world," "sweetness that never satiates" and "true bread of life."[67]

> **MACARIUS** – sometimes called Macarius the Great – was one of the most significant Desert Fathers in Egypt in the fourth century.

This formula – "Our Lord Jesus, the Christ, have mercy on me" – or a variation of it, became known as the Jesus Prayer. It is sometimes referred to as Prayer of the Heart. This particular prayer has been more popular in the Orthodox Church than in the Catholic Tradition. However, it has resurfaced in the Catholic Tradition thanks to the popularity of a little book entitled, *The Way of a Pilgrim*.[68]

John Cassian provides us with a similar expression of the same *monologistos* prayer form:

> This, then, is the devotional formula proposed to you as absolutely necessary for possessing the perpetual awareness of God: 'O God, incline unto my aid; O Lord, make haste to help me' (Ps 70:1).[69]

> **JOHN CASSIAN** was born in 360 and died in 435. After a number of years visiting the Desert Fathers in Egypt, he retired to Marseille, where he was the founder and first abbot of the St Victor Monastery.

St Benedict[70] who was significantly influenced by John Cassian, does not lay out any particular method of prayer in his *Rule*. However, over and above a number of references to communal and liturgical prayer – "the Work of God" – Benedict makes significant comments like, "every time you begin a good work you must pray to him to bring it to perfection" (prologue), "listen to holy reading and devote yourself often to prayer" (chapter 4:55–56) and "after the Work of God, all should leave (the oratory) in complete silence, and with reverence for God, so that a brother who may wish to pray alone will not be disturbed by the insensitivity of another" (chapter 52:2–3). Perhaps no statement in Benedict's *Rule* is more telling, however, than when he says the Cellarer "will regard all utensils and goods of the monastery as sacred vessels of the altar, aware that nothing is to be neglected" (chapter 31:10–11).

People raised in the Catholic Tradition prior to the Second Vatican Council (1962–65), were commonly taught to recall brief prayer formulae as they went about the business of the day. Thus, they might repeat "Jesus I love you" or "Jesus, Mary and Joseph, I give you my heart and my soul" or when passing a church or genuflecting in the church, "Jesus in the Blessed Sacrament I adore you". There were various prayers before and after meals, and prayers to begin and end the day. The Rosary was a common, simple form of prayer involving a set of beads – from the Old English word *bede* meaning "prayer" – that many carried in a pocket or handbag. (See chapter 15 for a further discussion of different prayer forms in the Catholic Tradition.)

In the fourteenth century the simple *monologistos* prayer was made the particular focus of a classic work, *The Cloud of Unknowing*. The anonymous author of this work writes:

> For a simple reaching out directly towards God is sufficient, without any other cause except himself. If you like, you can have this reaching out, wrapped up and enfolded in a single word. So as to have a better grasp of it, take just a little word, of one syllable rather than of two; for the shorter it is the better it is in agreement with this exercise of the spirit. Such a one is the word "God" or the word "love." Choose which one you prefer, or any other according to your liking – the word of one syllable that you like best.[70]

St Benedict of Nursia was born at Nursia, Italy in 480 and died at Monte Cassino Monastery in 547. Benedict is a towering figure in the Catholic Tradition. Apart from his remarkable *Rule*, he is generally regarded as the Father of Western monasticism.

John Main OSB was born in London in 1926. He died in 1982 of cancer. In 1975 Dom John began Christian meditation groups which met at Ealing Abbey, his monastery in West London, England and, later, in Montreal, Canada. These were the origins of the ecumenical network of Christian meditation groups which have become the World Community for Christian Meditation (WCCM). Check the internet for further information.

A rediscovery of this simple approach to prayer has occurred within the Catholic Church since the Second Vatican Council. Benedictine monk Fr John Main in the 1970s began to promote a form of "meditation" based particularly on the teachings of John Cassian. (See chapter 15 for more details.)

There is another form of prayer that has become popular in the last fifty years and can be mentioned here, though it is not strictly *monologistos* prayer. This form of prayer, promoted particularly by Cistercian monk Thomas Keating OCSO, is called Centering Prayer. It begins with *lectio divina* (See Chapter 7) – especially as experienced in the liturgy of the Word – and proceeds towards quiet, wordless reflection, opening into contemplation. There is a lot of material on Centering Prayer available on the internet. Centering Prayer depends very specifically on the doctrine of the indwelling Trinity. (See Chapter 15 for more details.)

There is a need for knowledge of the great truths of the faith to give this *monologistos* prayer its Christian grounding, shape and orientation.

For reflection

Take each text on its own and read it slowly and reflectively. Listen with the ear of the heart. Pause from time to time and listen to any movement within, whether it be a movement of resonance or resistance. Allow one word or phrase to emerge and chew that over, listening attentively within as you do so.

"In the first place it should be known that if a person is seeking God, his Beloved is seeking him much more. And if a soul directs to God its loving desires, … God sends it the fragrance of His ointments by which he draws it and makes it run after Him, and these are His divine inspirations and touches."[71]

"When we cry, 'Abba! Father!' it is that very Spirit bearing witness with our spirit that we are children of God, and if children, then heirs, heirs of God and joint heirs with Christ." (Rom 8:15-17)

O give thanks to the LORD, for he is good;
his steadfast love endures forever!
Let Israel say,
"His steadfast love endures forever."
Let the house of Aaron say,
"His steadfast love endures forever."
Let those who fear the LORD say,
"His steadfast love endures forever."
(Ps 118:1-4)

"'If you knew the gift of God!' (Jn 4:10). The wonder of prayer is revealed beside the well where we come seeking water: there, Christ comes to meet every human being. It is he who first seeks us and asks us for a drink. Jesus thirsts; his asking arises from the depths of God's desire for us. Whether we realize it or not, prayer is the encounter of God's thirst with ours. God thirsts that we may thirst for God." (CCC 2560)

For practice

In the coming days, recall a word or phrase from the Gospels or Psalms repeatedly as you go about the business of your day.

Some examples from the Gospels might be: "Jesus, Son of David, have mercy on me" (Mk 10:47); "My Lord and my God" (Jn 20:28); "Come and see" (Jn 1:39); "Abide in my love" (Jn 15:9); "I am the Way, the Truth and the Life" (Jn 14:6); and "Father, into your hands I commend my spirit" (Lk 23:46).

Some examples from the Psalms might be: "Be still and know that I am God" (Ps 46:10); "Be still before the Lord, and wait patiently for him" (Ps 37:7); and "When I look at your heavens, the work of your fingers, the moon and the stars that you have established; what are human beings that you are mindful of them, mortals that you care for them?" (Ps 8:3–4).

Each time you think of it, say a word of praise or thanks to God for something before you.

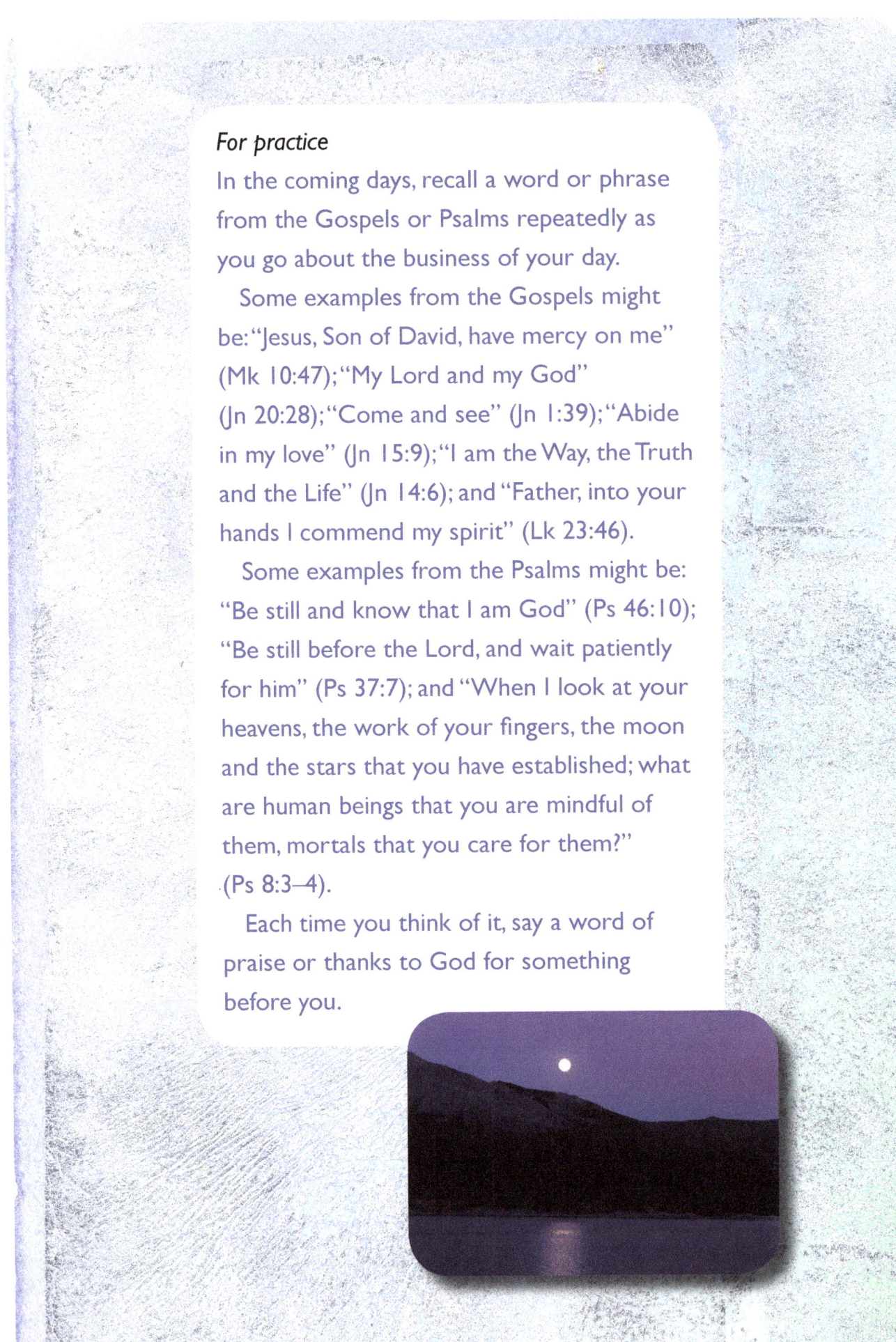

13

A moral life

*"For then will be brought to fruition in us that prayer of our Savior
which he prayed to his Father on his disciples' behalf when he said:
'The love with which you have loved me may be in them, and they in us' (Jn 17:26).
And again: 'That all may be one, as you Father in me and I in you,
that they may also be one in us' (Jn 17:21).
Then that perfect love of God, by which 'he loved us first' (1 Jn 4:10),
will also have passed into our heart's disposition upon the fulfilment of this prayer of the Lord,
which we believe can in no way be rendered void.
This will be the case when every love, every desire,
every effort, every undertaking, every thought of ours,
everything that we live, that we speak, that we breathe, will be God,
and when that unity which the Father now has with the Son and which the Son
has with the Father will be carried over into our understanding and our mind,
so that, just as he loves us with a sincere and pure and indissoluble love,
we too may be joined to him with a perpetual and inseparable love
and so united with him that whatever we breathe, whatever we understand,
whatever we speak, may be God."*[72]

The prayerful life is one with the moral life. We could sum it up this way: "As you have been loved into freedom by God, be in the world in such a way that God may love others into freedom through you."

We are called to be in love – literally, to *be in love*. Love is the beginning, end and meaning of our existence. The prayerful life and the moral life both work towards the ultimate fulfilment of our beings as creatures made in the image and likeness of God as infinite love. Thomas Merton writes:

> To say I am made in the image and likeness of God is to say that love is the reason for my existence, for God is love. … Love is my true identity. Selflessness is my true self. Love is my true character. Love is my name.[73]

We must respond. There is work to be done. The advice given to travellers may in fact get to the heart of the matter: travel light! If the road to hell is paved with good intentions, the road to heaven is surely strewn with useless baggage. John of the Cross, for example, is typical of the Tradition in emphasising detachment. And he reminds us that *any* attachment is an obstacle to the experience of the deeper delights of love and the fulfilment of our best possibilities: "It makes little difference whether a bird is tied by a thin thread or by a cord."[74]

Detachment leads to freedom and joy:

> The kingdom of heaven is like treasure hidden in a field, which someone found and hid; then in his joy he goes and sells all that he has and buys that field. (Mt 13:44)

Detachment is also a necessary part of moving beyond selfishness and greed, beyond resentment and the inability to forgive, and beyond injustice and hatred. Those who know they are loved infinitely – know it in their bones! – are no longer so vulnerable to the impulses that lead us to feel a need to be selfish, greedy, resentful, unable to forgive, inclined to injustice and hatred. Their inclination is, rather, towards altruism, generosity, forgiveness, acts of justice and love. These latter expressions come, not so much as acts of will but as gifts, not so much as stoic conquests but as God's grace.

For reflection

Take each text on its own and read it slowly and reflectively. Listen with the ear of the heart. Pause from time to time and listen to any movement within, whether it be a movement of resonance or resistance. Is there anything in your life that is an obstacle to love?

"'God is love, and he who abides in love abides in God, and God abides in him' (1 Jn 4:16). These words from the First Letter of John express with remarkable clarity the heart of the Christian faith: the Christian image of God and the resulting image of humankind and its destiny. In the same verse, Saint John also offers a kind of summary of the Christian life: 'We have come to know and to believe in the love God has for us.' *We have come to believe in God's love*: in these words the Christian can express the fundamental decision of his or her life. Being Christian is not the result of an ethical choice or a lofty idea, but the encounter with an event, a person, which gives life a new horizon and a decisive direction. Saint John's Gospel describes that event in these words: 'God so loved the world that he gave his only Son, that whoever believes in him should ... have eternal life' (3:16)."[75]

"This is my commandment, that you love one another as I have loved you. No one has greater love than this, to lay down one's life for one's friends. You are my friends if you do what I command you. I do not call you servants any longer, because the servant does not know what the master is doing; but I have called you friends, because I have made known to you everything that I have heard from my Father. You did not choose me but I chose you. And I appointed you to go and bear fruit, fruit that will last, so that the Father will give you whatever you ask him in my name. I am giving you these commands so that you may love one another." (2 Jn 15:12-17)

"He has told you, O mortal, what is good; and what does the Lord require of you but to do justice, and to love kindness, and to walk humbly with your God?" (Mic 6:8)

"And so our good Lord answered to all the questions and doubts which I could raise, saying more comfortingly: I may make all things well, and I can make all things well, and I shall make all things well, and I will make all things well; and you will see yourself that every kind of thing will be well. When he says 'I may', I understand this to apply to the Father; and when he says 'I can', I understand it for the Son; and when I says 'I will', I understand if for the Holy Spirit; and when he says 'I shall', I understand it for the unity of the blessed Trinity, three persons and one truth; and when he says 'You will see yourself', I understand it for the union of all men who will be saved in the blessed Trinity. And in these five words God wishes us to be enclosed in rest and in peace. And so Christ's spiritual thirst will have an end. For this is Christ's spiritual thirst, his longing in love, which persists and always will, until we see him on the day of judgment, for we who shall be saved and shall be Christ's joy and bliss are still here, and some are yet to come, and so will some be until that day. Therefore this is his thirst and longing in love for us, to gather us all here into him, to our endless joy, as I see it. For we are not now so wholly in him as we then shall be."[76]

For practice

Accompany yourself through the coming days, as a very good friend might. Pay particular attention to moments when you are inclined to pass moral judgment on someone. Such judgments can be autobiographical. Listen to the emotions associated with the judgment. Ask the open question: what is going on here?

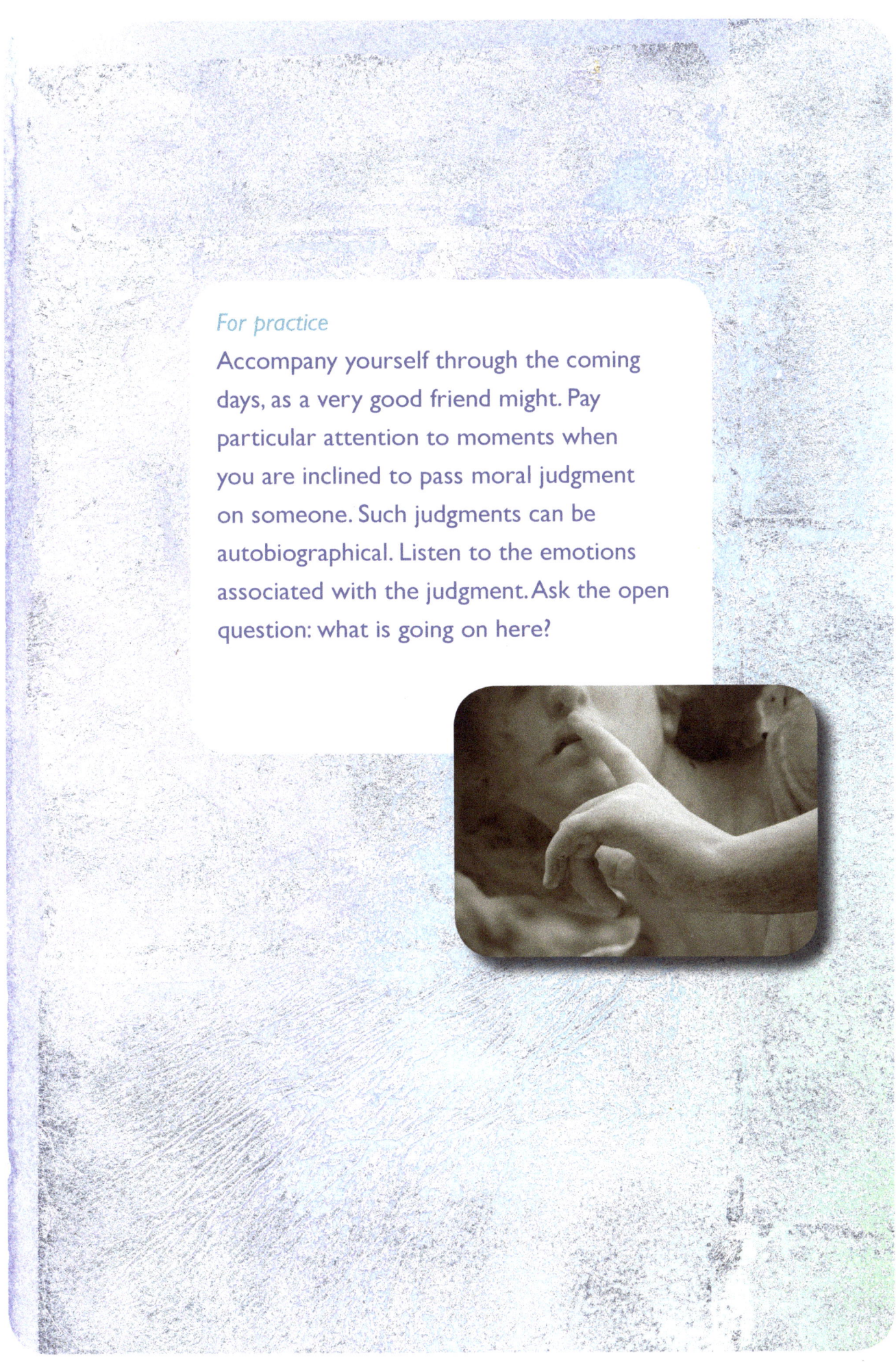

14
Discipline

*"To be, to be possessed of the gift of life and to be granted all that makes its richness
means to be loved by God; and those who know this, free from any delusion that they can exist
or possess apart from this mystery of love have entered into the Kingdom of God which is the Kingdom of
Love. What then shall be their response to this generous, self-effacing, sacrificial Love?
An endeavour to respond to love for love, as there is no other way of acknowledging love.
And this response is the ascetic endeavour, which can be summed up in the words of the Lord Jesus Christ:
'Renounce yourself, take up your Cross and follow Me.'
To recognize one's own nonentity and discover the secret of the Kingdom is not enough:
the King of Love must be enthroned in our mind and heart, take undivided possession of our will
and make of our very bodies the temples of the Holy Ghost.
This small particle of the cosmos which is our soul and body must be conquered,
freed by a lifelong struggle from enslavement to the world and to the devil,
freed as if it were an occupied country and restored to its legitimate King. . . .
(and this process) is not rooted in an hypocritical
or contrived depreciation of self, but in the vision of God,
and a humbling experience of being so loved."*[77]

The Desert Fathers and Mothers were "men and women wrapped in a depth of inner silence of which we have no idea and who taught by 'being,' not by speech."[78] Their very lives became a living witness to that Presence in the world. They could have said with St Paul: "It is no longer I who live, but it is Christ who lives in me." (Gal 2:20) Which reminds us of Jesus' own words to Philip about his being with us: "Do you not believe that I am in the Father and the Father is in me? The words that I say to you I do not speak on my own; but the Father who dwells in me does his works." (Jn 14:10)

When we see ballet dancers glide across the stage, although it might appear effortless in its grace, we would not dare suggest to those ballet dancers that there is no effort, even pain, underlying what they do. The well-trained and talented ballet dancer knows in and through the body where and how to move, and he or she has the freedom to actually move in that way.

This demands discipline. The English word *discipline* has its roots in the Latin word *discipulus* meaning "disciple". Discipline, in the best sense of the word means *to make a disciple of*. Thus, the ballet dancer makes disciples of the inherent talent, the muscles, tendons and joints, the mind and emotions, and so on, so there is an integration and coherence as all the human energies of the organism combine in their presence on the stage. The result is the physical grace and freedom we love to watch.

The actions we take in the process of making disciples of our energies – whether it is to be present on stage as a ballet dancer or present to the Presence – are of two kinds. On the one hand, we *choose* actions and behaviours that will facilitate the end we seek, on the other hand, we *avoid* actions and behaviours that will obstruct the end we seek.

The result of these actions, if well conceived, is twofold:

Knowledge— in our very beings, especially in our bodies, we come to know what must be done. We acquire a knowledge beyond the merely rational, a knowledge that no longer requires deliberation; it is like instinct.

54 A Friendly Guide to Prayer

Freedom —we are able to act on that knowledge and achieve the desired ends which are in accord with our talents and capabilities.

Typically, the efforts of training and discipline in all of the great religious traditions focus broadly on three interrelated areas:

firstly, freedom from *physical* compulsions relating to bodily appetites (notably, concerning food, drink, sleep, sex, speech, movement and posture), so that there is a growing knowledge in and through the body of what matters and a bodily freedom in service of deeper things

secondly, freedom from *psychological* compulsions (notably, anxiety/fear and the consequent desire to control, which can lead us, in turn, to be preoccupied with gathering power through possessions, status, role, knowledge, game playing and various strategies and tactics, and so on) so that there is a growing knowledge deep in our psyches and a psychological freedom in service of deeper things

thirdly, freedom from *spiritual* compulsions (notably, pride which can lead us to make idols of ourselves, our opinions, our organisation, and so on) so that there is growing spiritual knowledge and spiritual freedom in service of our openness to the Divine.

All of the above apply to our efforts to become prayerful. It will require a measure of discipline. There is no other way. We should realise, however, that any pain or discomfort we might experience in this discipline will be associated with the loss of some delight – something that comforts, satisfies or pleases us and/or lends a sense of security to our lives – that in fact is less than the delight that awaits us. We are built for delight. We will necessarily seek delight. We should never settle for less than the greatest delight of all, the fulfilment of the soul's deepest longing, our being in love.

For reflection

Take each text on its own and read it slowly and reflectively. Listen with the ear of the heart. Pause from time to time and listen to any movement within, whether it be a movement of resonance or resistance. Pay particular attention to the ambiguities and/or doubts that arise within.

"A brother said to Abbot Pastor: If I give one of my brothers a little bread or something of the sort, the demons spoil everything and it seems to me that I have acted only to please men. The elder said to him: Even if your good work was done to please, we must still give to our brothers and sisters what they need. And he told him this story. Two farmers lived in a village. One of them sowed his seed and reaped only a small and wretched crop. The other neglected to sow anything at all, and so he reaped nothing. Which of the two will survive if there is a famine? The brother replied: The first one, even though his crop is small and wretched. The elder said to him: Let us also sow, even though our sowing is small and wretched, lest we die in the time of hunger."[79]

"Be watchful and unsleeping in spirit. Address yourself to people personally, as is the way of God himself, and carry the infirmities of them all on your own shoulders, as a good champion of Christ ought to do. … There is no credit in spending all your affections on the cream of your pupils. Try rather to bring the more troublesome ones to order, by using gentleness. Nobody can heal every wound with the same unguent; where there are acute spasms of pain, we have to apply soothing poultices. So in all circumstances be as wise as the serpent, though always harmless as the dove."[80]

"Like a city breached, without walls, is one who lacks self-control." (Prov 25:28)

"It is the God who said, 'Let light shine out of darkness,' who has shone in our hearts to give the light of the knowledge of the glory of God in the face of Jesus Christ. But we have this treasure in clay jars, so that it may be made clear that this extraordinary power belongs to God and does not come from us." (2 Cor 4:6-7)

For practice

Pay close attention to yourself in the coming days, taking note of any attachments you might have in your life. Be gentle, non-judgmental but ruthlessly honest as you listen to what is going on there. Would it be good if you responded in some way? Be gentle. Do not hurry.

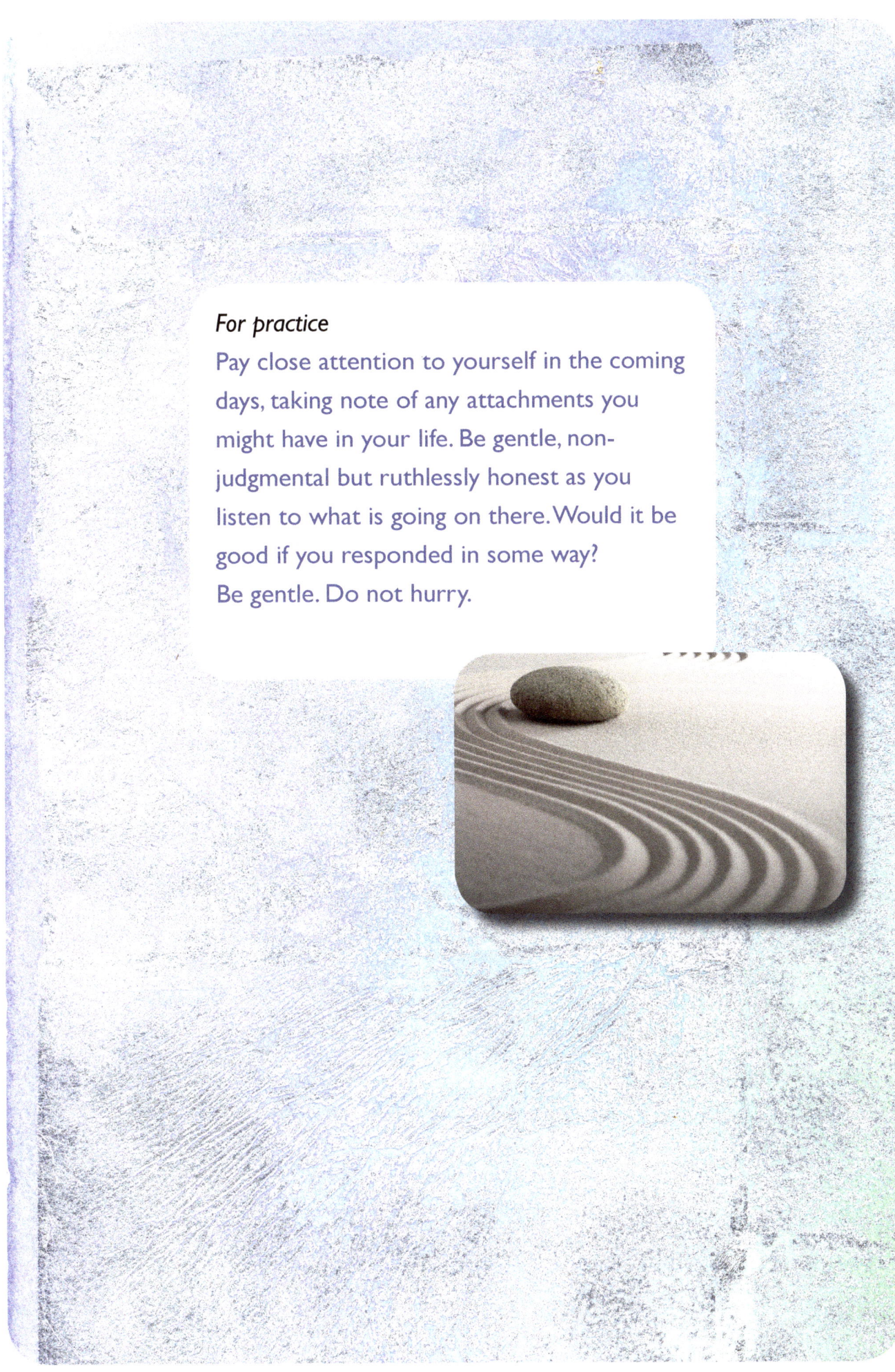

15
Some Catholic practices

The journey towards greater prayerfulness is also a journey towards unity – with God, self, other people and the rest of creation. The more deeply we live this human vocation, the more we tend to think "we" rather than "I", "us" rather than "me", "ours" rather than "mine". Spirituality is inherently a social reality. So is prayer. Both, if authentic, draw us out of ourselves towards the world so loved by God (see Jn 3:16).

The Catholic Tradition of prayer reflects this. The primary form of prayer is communal prayer. The community of the baptised come together – in the early Church the Greek word *ekklesia* meaning "assembly" or "gathering" was used for this coming together. Even when we pray on our own, we pray on behalf of the community as members of the Body of Christ. The hermit and the monk or nun bear witness to the Body of Christ. They are not disconnected individuals, even if they do live apart.

Over and above the liturgy, the formal prayer of the Church and the primary prayer for Catholics, there are a number of practices, rituals and prayers that are designed to promote remembrance and awareness thus preventing us from slipping into lives of forgetfulness in the busyness of our days.

Number 2698 of the *Catechism of the Catholic Church* states that "the Tradition of the Church proposes to the faithful certain rhythms of praying intended to nourish continual prayer". In the same place in the *Catechism* we find encouragement to engage in the "basic rhythms of the Christian life of prayer". What follows are a few practices that facilitate this process.

The sign of the Cross

The sign of the Cross is signified by a movement of the right hand to the forehead, down to the stomach, up to the left shoulder and across to the right shoulder, normally accompanied by the words, "In the name of the Father, and of the Son and of the Holy Spirit". In this way a central symbol of the faith is ritually traced on our bodies. We are reminded of the Paschal Mystery and the triumph of love over hate, truth over lies, and good over evil. We are also reminded of the Blessed Trinity and that God is a community of love. This ritual normally begins and ends other prayers.

The Our Father

A simple recitation of the words Jesus suggested when the disciples asked him to teach them how to prayer: "Our Father, who art in heaven, hallowed by Thy name. Thy Kingdom come. They will be done, on earth as it is in heaven. Give us this day our daily bread and forgive us our trespasses as we forgive those who trespass against us. And lead us not into temptation but deliver us from evil" (see Matthew 6:9–14). This prayer expresses the essence

58 A Friendly Guide to Prayer

of our relationships with God, self, other people and the world. It may be said on its own. It is often said in conjunction with other prayers, such as the Hail Mary (see The Rosary and The Angelus below).

The Hail Mary

An expression of Mary's disposition, willing to play her part in the Incarnation as the Mother of Jesus: "Hail Mary full of grace. The Lord is with you. Blessed are you among women and blessed is the fruit of your womb, Jesus. Holy Mary, Mother of God, pray for us sinners now and at the hour of our death. Amen" (see Lk 1:28 and 42). By the end of the third century, Mary had become known by the Greek title *Theotokos*, which can mean either "God-bearer" or "Mother of God". The first part of the Hail Mary – known by its Latin words *Ave Maria* – was a common devotional prayer in the twelfth century. The second part of the prayer – beginning "Holy Mary" – was added in the sixteenth century (see The Rosary and The Angelus below).

Glory be to the Father

"Glory be to the Father, and to the Son and to the Holy Spirit. As it was in the beginning, is now and ever shall be, world without end. Amen." A prayer said at the conclusion of the recitation of the Psalms in The Prayer of the Church, but also used commonly elsewhere to conclude prayers generally. We are reminded of the Trinity, the eternal community that is God. We are also reminded to keep our lives in perspective, always thinking of ourselves, other people and our world against the backdrop of God's eternal love (see The Rosary and The Angelus below).

Apostles' Creed

A summary of Christian belief in twelve statements that had gained currency by the end of the fourth century: "I believe in God, the Father almighty, creator of heaven and earth. I believe in Jesus Christ, his only Son, our Lord. He was conceived by the power of the Holy Spirit and born of the Virgin Mary. He suffered under Pontius Pilate, was crucified, died, and was buried. He descended to the dead. On the third day he rose again. He extended into heaven and is seated at the right hand of the Father. He will come again to judge the living and the dead. I believe in the Holy Spirit, the holy Catholic Church, the communion of saints, the forgiveness of sins, the ressurection of the body, and life everlasting. Amen"[81] (see The Rosary below).

The Rosary

The Rosary consists of the recitation of five sets of ten "Hail Marys", preceded by an "Our Father" and concluding with a "Glory be to the Father". After the apparitions of Mary in Fatima, Portugal, in 1917, it became customary to add the so-called Fatima Prayer after the "Glory be to the Father": "O my Jesus, forgive us our sins, save us from the fires of hell. Lead/bring all souls to heaven, especially those most in need of your mercy". Normally, before the five sets of "Hail Marys", the Rosary begins with the sign of the Cross, the prayer from the Prayer of the Church, "O Lord open my lips. My mouth shall declare your praise", the Apostle's Creed, one "Our Father" followed by three "Hail Marys" in honour of the Blessed Trinity and one "Glory be to the Father".

The five sets of ten "Hail Marys" may lead to a meditation on the five Joyful Mysteries – Annunciation (Lk 1:28), Visitation (Lk 1:41–42), Nativity (Lk 2:7), Presentation in the Temple (Lk 2:22–23) and Finding the Child Jesus in the Temple (Lk 2:46) – or the five Sorrowful Mysteries – Agony in the Garden (Lk 22:44–45), Scourging at the Pillar (Jn 19:1), Crowning with Thorns (Mt 27:28–29), Carrying of the Cross (Jn 19:17) and Crucifixion (Lk 23:46) – or the five Glorious Mysteries – Resurrection (Mk 16:6), Ascension (Mk 16:19), Descent of the Holy Spirit (Acts 2:4), Assumption of Our Lady into Heaven (Rev 12:1) and Coronation of our Lady Queen of Heaven (Jdt 15:9–11) – or the five Mysteries of Light – Christ's Baptism (Mk 1:10), Christ's Self-Revelation at Cana (Jn 2:11), Christ's Proclamation of the Kingdom (Mk 1:15), Christ's Transfiguration (Mt 17:2) and Christ's Institution of the Eucharist (Lk 22:19).

A set of beads is normally used to count off the various prayers. Sets of beads are normally blessed by a priest. The English word "Rosary" comes from the Latin word *rosarium* meaning "rose garden", being a general term for a collection of similar points. Later mythology used the rose as a symbol of joy and came to associate it with Mary the Mother of Jesus. The Rosary as a popular prayer seems to have come into being about the early fifteenth century, evolving from various practices of recitation of "Our Fathers" and "Hail Marys".

The Angelus

The Angelus is a prayer – so named after the opening word of the Latin – said daily at 6 a.m., noon and 6 p.m. in honour of the Incarnation. Although known in late medieval times – St Bonaventure (1221–1274) introduced the ringing of the Angelus bell to remember the Incarnation – The Angelus did not become widespread until the seventeenth century. The prayer is as follows:

> The Angel of the Lord declared to Mary:
> And she conceived of the Holy Spirit.
> Hail Mary, full of grace etc. (see above)
> Behold the handmaid of the Lord:
> Be it done unto me according to Your word.
> Hail Mary etc.
> And the Word was made Flesh:
> And dwelt among us.
> Hail Mary etc.
> Pray for us, O Holy Mother of God:
> That we may be made worthy of the promises of Christ.
> Let us pray:
> Pour forth, we beseech You, O Lord, Your grace into our hearts; that we, to whom the incarnation of Christ, Your Son, was made known by the message of an angel, may by His Passion and Cross be brought to the glory of His Resurrection, through the same Christ Our Lord.

All prayer helps us to remember who and what and why we are. Living in forgetfulness is a tragedy. Specific prayers such as The Angelus help us to remember that God so loved the world he gave his only Son (see Jn 3:16).

Holy Water

Water is blessed in a formal ritual and kept in a receptacle near the entrance to the church. It is also sometimes kept in homes. On entering a church, we dip our fingers in the holy water font and make the sign of the Cross. Holy water is used for various blessings, such as the blessing of the coffin at a funeral. Water is a simple element of our daily lives, used for both drinking and washing. This twofold meaning is also present in the prayerful use of Holy Water. We are reminded of our Baptism, of the fact that life comes to us as gift and that we all need to be cleansed of all that stands between us and the Kingdom of God.

Genuflection

The right knee is bent to touch the floor. A ritual of reverence, normally reserved for entering and leaving a church where the Blessed Sacrament is reserved. We are reminded that God is God, our Creator and Redeemer. Sometimes a brief silent prayer – for example, "Jesus in the Blessed Sacrament I adore you" – is said in accompaniment to the genuflection.

Morning offering

At the beginning of the day a prayer is said to acknowledge the Presence of God and to place the day in God's hands. Various forms of this offering may be used. An example is: "I offer you God my prayers, works, joys, and sufferings of this day for all the intentions of Your Sacred Heart, in union with the Holy Sacrifice of the Mass throughout the world, in reparation for my sins, for the intentions of our Holy Father this month. Amen."

Examination of conscience

At the end of the day a few minutes are taken to reflect on the day. We may give thanks for the gifts in the day, praise for the Presence of God, sorrow for not having been more available to God or for some word or deed that was less loving than it could have been, we may pray for God's blessing on someone in particular and finally we may place our life and the lives of others in the hands of God.

Prayer before meals

An example of a prayer before a meal is: "Bless us O Lord and these your gifts which of your bounty we are about to receive. Through Christ our Lord. Amen." This prayer may be opened and closed with the sign of the Cross.

Prayer after meals

An example of a prayer after a meal is: "We give you thanks for all your gifts Almighty God. You live and reign forever and ever. Amen." This prayer may be opened and closed with the sign of the Cross.

Spontaneous prayers

The day will normally contain many moments when it is appropriate to pray spontaneously. Sometimes this is done according to a brief formula – like "Jesus I love you" or "Jesus, Mary and Joseph, I give you my heart and my soul" – or according to a more conversational style appropriate to the moment – perhaps expressing joy or praise, seeking strength or wisdom, or perhaps just recalling a word or phrase from the Gospels.

The Jesus Prayer

"Lord Jesus Christ, Son of God, have mercy on me" is a prayer formula that became common practice in the early centuries. It was a response to St Paul's urging: "Pray without ceasing" (1 Thess 5:16–19), drawing on the belief in the power of the name of Jesus and taking inspiration from the blind man, Bartimaeus: "Jesus, Son of David, have mercy on me!" (Lk 18:38). The Jesus Prayer is to be gently repeated continually, until it moves beyond the lips and becomes a prayer of the heart. It can be prayed when you sit down for a dedicated time of prayer or when you are busy about the duties of your day. It can be brought into consciousness when you are under stress or need special wisdom for a particular moment. The Jesus Prayer opens us to the Presence in the depths of our being. It allows the love, truth, goodness and beauty of God to pervade our consciousness. It brings peace and perspective.

The Jesus Prayer, when it becomes the prayer of the heart, is perpetual, helping us to live in remembrance, always available to respond to life's invitations and challenges according to the Holy Spirit. The Jesus Prayer takes us beyond the words of the prayer into silence; we become present to the Presence. It has done its job when you forget that it is there, silently expressing your heart's deepest desire (see the chapter on "Simplicity" for further background on the Jesus Prayer).

Centering prayer

This is how Fr Thomas Keating OCSO, the founder of the Centering Prayer Movement, describes it:

To do this systematically, take up a comfortable position that will enable you to sit still. Close your eyes. Half of the world disappears for we generally think about what we see. In order to slow down the usual flow of thoughts, think just one thought. For this purpose choose a word of one or two syllables with which you feel comfortable as a gesture or symbol of your consent to God's presence and action within you during periods of centering prayer.

A general loving look toward God may be better suited to the disposition of some persons. In either case, the same procedures are followed as in the use of the sacred word. The word is sacred because it is the symbol of your intention to consent to God's presence beyond thoughts, images, and emotions. It is chosen not for its content but for its intent.

To start, silently introduce the sacred word as gently as if you were laying a feather on a piece of absorbent cotton. The sacred word is not meant to be repeated continuously. It can become vague or just an impulse of the will, or even disappear.

Some Catholic practices 61

When you become aware that you are thinking about or engaged with some thought, return to the sacred word as the expression of your intent. The effectiveness of this prayer does not depend on how distinctly you say the sacred word or how often, but rather on the gentleness with which you introduce it in the beginning and the promptness with which you return to it when you are engaged mentally or emotionally with some thought.

Thoughts are a normal, inevitable, and integral part of centering prayer. Our ordinary thoughts are like boats sitting on a river so closely packed together that we cannot see the river that is holding them up. A 'thought' in the context of this prayer is any perception that arises in consciousness, whether a body sensation, feeling emotion, image, memory, plan, concept, reflection, psychological breakthrough, or spiritual experience. We are normally aware of one object after another passing across the inner screen of consciousness. When we pay no attention to that flow, space begins to appear, between the boats. Up comes the reality on which they are floating.

Centering prayer is a method of directing your attention from the particular to the general, from the concrete to the formless. At first you are preoccupied by the particular 'boats' that are going by. You become interested in seeing what is on them. But just let them all go by. If you notice you are becoming interested in them, return to the sacred word as the gift of your whole being to God present within you.[82]

Maranatha is an Aramaic word found in 1 Corinthians 16:22 and is generally translated "The Lord is coming" or "Lord, come!". The word is filled with the hope and expectation of Jesus' return and the fulness of the Kingdom of God.

Christian meditation

This is how Fr John Main OSB, the founder of the Christian meditation movement describes it:

> Sit down. Sit still and upright. Close your eyes lightly. Sit relaxed but alert. Silently, interiorly, begin to say a single word. We recommend the prayer phrase, *maranatha*. Recite it as four syllables of equal length. Listen to it as you say it, gently but continuously. Do not think or imagine anything – spiritual or otherwise. If thoughts and images come, these are distractions at the time of meditation, so keep returning to simply saying the word. Meditate each morning and evening for between twenty and thirty minutes.[83]

Prayer of petition

Prayer is frequently a way of making a specific request. We find this throughout the liturgy as well as in personal prayer. The Lord's Prayer is paradigmatic in this regard (see Mt 6:7–15; Lk 11:2–4). Jesus tells his disciple to "ask and it will be given to you" (see Mt 7:7–11; Lk 11:9–13; Mk 11:24). Jesus repeatedly responds to requests from individuals (see Mt 8:5–13; Lk 7:1–10; Jn 4:46–53) and even encourages some to make their request known (see Mk 10:46–52). Jesus asks the Father to "let this cup pass" in the Garden of Gethsemane (see Mk 14:36; Mt 26:39; Lk 22:42). In the latter instance Jesus adds an important rider: "Not my will but your will be done". This is the key. We pray prayers of petition because Jesus did and because he asked us to pray these prayers. We do not pray them because they "work".

Endnotes

1 Evagrius of Pontus (346–399) cited by Kallistos Ware, *The Orthodox Way*, Mowbray's, 1979, 54.
2 Adrian van Kaam, *Studies in Formative Spirituality*, I, 2 (1980), 303.
3 Cited in Charles Cummings, *Monastic Practices*, Cistercian Publications, 1986, 9. (See Rainer Maria Rilke, *The Notebooks of Malte Laurids Brigge*, translated by M D Herter Norton and W W Norton, 1949, 201.)
4 Aelred Squire, *Asking the Fathers*, SPCK, 1973/1994, 20.
5 *The Sayings of the Desert Fathers*, translated by Benedicta Ward SLG, Mowbray, 1981, 6.
6 Adrian van Kaam, *Religion and Personality*, Image Books, 1964/1968, 24.
7 Walker Percy in Patrick Samway, editor, *Walker Percy: Signposts in a Strange Land*, Farrar, Straus and Giroux, 1991, 417.
8 Adrian van Kaam, *Religion and Personality*, Image Books, 1964/1968, 24.
9 Blaise Pascal, *Pensées*, J M Dent & Sons, 59.
10 Karl Rahner, "The Question of the Future", *Theological Investigations 12*, Darton Longman & Todd, 1974, 189.
11 Abraham Heschel, *God in Search of Man: A Philosophy of Judaism*, Farrar, Straus & Giroux, 1955/1978, 64.
12 *Summa Theologica*, I, q12, a7.
13 *Summa Theologica*, I, q12, a13, ad1.
14 St Augustine, *Sermon*, LII, vi, 16.
15 St Gregory of Nyssa, *The Life of Moses*, Chapters 162–163, translated by Abraham Malherbe and Everett Ferguson, *Gregory of Nyssa: The Life of Moses*, Paulist Press, 1978, 94–95.
16 Pierre-Marie Delfieux, *The Jerusalem Community Rule of Life*, 12–13. See the web site: http://jerusalem.cef.fr/jerusalem/en/en_13livrevie.html.
17 John Courtney Murray, *The Problem of God: Yesterday and Today*, Yale University Press, 1964/1977, 10f.
18 Dorothy Day, "During World War II", in Shawn Madigan, editor, *Mystics, Visionaries and Prophets: A Historical Anthology of Women's Mystical Writings*, Fortress Press, 1998, 355.
19 Hans Kung, *On Being a Christian*, Doubleday, 1976, 410.
20 Thomas Merton, *The New Man*, Farrar Straus Giroux, 1961, 193–194.
21 John Dominic Crossan, *In Parables: The Challenge of the Historical Jesus*, Harper and Row, 1973, 82.
22 From St Gregory Nazianzen's eulogy for his friend, St Basil of Caesarea. Gregory is actually quoting Basil himself. Cited by Olivier Clément, *The Roots of Christian Mysticism*, translated by Theodore Berkeley OCSO and Jeremy Hummerstone, New City Press, 1982/1995, 76.
23 *Against Heresies*, III:10, 2. Cited by Olivier Clément, op cit, 89.
24 Pseudo-Macarius, *Great Letter*, cited in Olivier Clément, op cit, 89–90.
25 Gregory of Nyssa, *Homilies on the Beatitudes,* 6 (PG 44, 1270). Cited by Olivier Clément, op cit, 237.
26 *Presbyterorum Ordinis* (Decree on the Life and Ministry of Priests), 6.
27 St Augustine, *Sermon 272*, cited by Nathan Mitchell, "Liturgy and Ecclesiology" in *Handbook for Liturgical Studies*, Volume II: Fundamental Liturgy, edited by Anscar J Chupungco OSB, The Liturgical Press, 1998, 124–125.

28 Thomas Merton, *The Road to Joy: The Letters of Thomas Merton to New and Old Friends*, edited by Robert E Daggy, Farrar, Straus, Giroux, 1989, 118.
29 Blaise Pascal, *Pensées*, translated by John Warrington, J M Dent & Sons, 1960/1973, 70.
30 Dorotheos of Gaza, *Discourses and Sayings*, translated by Eric P Wheeler, Cistercian Publications, 1977, 138–139.
31 A French saying, cited by Bob Lax in a conversation with Peter France, in Peter France, *Hermits: The Insights of Solitude*, St Martin's Griffin, 1996, 200.
32 Jean-Marie Howe OCSO, *Secret of the Heart: Spiritual Being*, Cistercian Publications, 2005, xiii.
33 Canon 214 from the 1983 Code of Canon Law.
34 Thomas Merton, *The Wisdom of the Desert*, New Directions, 1960, 26.
35 "Sermon One" in *Meister Eckhart: Sermons and Treatises*, Volume I, translated and edited by M O'C Walshe, Element Books, 1989, 33.
36 "Sermon Thirteen (b)" in *Meister Eckhart: Sermons and Treatises*, Volume I, op cit, 118.
37 St John Chrysostom, *Office of Readings*, Friday After Ash Wednesday.

38 Caryll Houselander cited in Maisie Ward, *The Divine Eccentric*, London 1943, 74. Cited by George Maloney, *The Breath of the Mystic*, Dimension Books, 1974, 185.
39 St Ignatius of Antioch, "Letter to the Ephesians" in Maxwell Staniforth, translator, *Early Christian Writings: The Apostolic Fathers*, Penguin Books, 1987, 63.
40 Cited in T E Pollard, *Johannine Christology and the Early Church*, Cambridge University Press, 1970, 19, footnote.
41 Owen Chadwick, editor, *Western Asceticism*, Westminster Press, 1958, 105.
42 Thomas Merton, editor, *The Wisdom of the Desert*, op cit, 63.
43 St Thomas Aquinas, *Summa Theologica*, IIa IIae, q25, a5, translated by the Fathers of the English Dominican Province, Christian Classics, 1981.
44 St Bernard of Clairvaux, *On The Song of Songs*, Sermon 19, translated by Kilian Walsh OCSO, Cistercian Publications, 1971, 146.

45 St Clement of Rome's "Letter to the Corinthians" in Maxwell Staniforth, translator, *Early Christian Writings*, Penguin, 1968/1982, 42.
46 *The Cloud of Unknowing*, Chapter III, James Walsh, SPCK, 1981, 119–121.
47 St John of the Cross, "The Living Flame of Love," 3:32 in *The Collected Works of St John of the Cross*, translated by Kieran Kavanaugh OCD and Otilio Rodriguez OCD, ICS Publications 1973, 622.
48 See for instance St John of the Cross, "The Living Flame of Love", 3:29–31, op cit, 620–621.
49 St John of the Cross, "The Living Flame of Love", 3:12–13, op cit, 583.
50 St Ignatius of Antioch, "Letter to the Ephesians" in Mawell Staniforth, op cit, 65.

51 Benedict XVI, *Caritas in Veritate* (Charity in Truth), 2.
52 John Henry Newman, *An Essay in Aid of a Grammar of Assent*, Longmans, Green and Company, 1870/1903, 89. See: http://www.newmanreader.org/works/grammar/.
53 See, for example, John Henry Newman, op cit, "Real Assent" and "Notional and Real Assent Contrasted".
54 See also St Teresa's *The Way of Perfection*, chapter 28, 9–10.

55 Week I, first exercise, first prelude.
56 Source unknown.
57 Graham Greene, *The Power and the Glory*, Penguin Books, 1971, 131. Recall a suggestion made earlier in this course: think of other people – *imagine* them – as tragic-comic stories like you.
58 Gustave Weigel, "How is the Council Going?", *America*, 109 (December 7, 1963), 730.
59 St Bernard of Clairvaux, *Sermon on the Song of Songs*, 69:7 in Irene Edmonds, translator, *St Bernard of Clairvaux on the Song of Songs IV*, Cistercian Publications, 1980, 34.
60 St Augustine, *City of God*, Book 14:9 in Whitney J Oates, translator, *Basic Writings of St Augustine, Volume II*, Random House, 1948, 250.
61 *Spiritual Exercises*, Second Annotation, op cit, 6.
62 *Spiritual Exercises*, Ninth Rule [322], op cit, 210.
63 St John of the Cross, *The Spiritual Canticle* in Kieran Kavanaugh OCD and Otilio Rodriguez, translators, *The Collected works of St John of the Cross*, Institute of Carmelite Studies, 1973, 417.
64 Diadochus of Photike, *Office of Readings*, Week 2 of Ordinary Time, Friday.
65 André Louf, *Teach Us To Pray*, Darton, Longman and Todd, 1974, 19.

66 Louis Bouyer, *A History of Christian Spirituality, Volume I: The Spirituality of the New Testament and the Fathers*, The Seabury Press, 1963, 376.
67 Cited in Louis Bouyer, op cit, 376–377.
68 See *The Way of a Pilgrim and The Pilgrim Continues His Way*, translated by R M French, Hope Publishing House, 1993.
69 John Cassian, *Tenth Conference: On Prayer*, X, 2, in Boniface Ramsey OP, translator, *John Cassian: The Conferences*, Paulist Press, 1997, 378.
70 *The Cloud of Unknowing*, op cit, Chapter VII, 133–134.
71 St John of the Cross, "The Living Flame of Love", 3:28, op cit, 620.
72 John Cassian, op cit, VII, 1–2, 376–377.
73 Thomas Merton, *New Seeds of Contemplation*, New Directions, 1972, 60.
74 St John of the Cross, "The Ascent of Mount Carmel", Book 1:4, op cit, 97.
75 Julian of Norwich, *Showings*, (Thirty First Chapter) translated by Edmund Colledge OSA and James Walsh SJ, Paulist Press, 1978, 229–230.
76 Pope Benedict XVI, *Deus Caritas Est* (December 25, 2005), 1.
77 Anthony of Sourozh, "Foreword" to Benedicta Ward SLG, *The Sayings of the Desert Fathers*, Mowbray, 1975/1981, viii–ix.
78 Ibid.
79 Thomas Merton, *The Wisdom of the Desert*, op cit, 51.
80 St Ignatius of Antioch writing to St Polycarp, Bishop of Smyrna, in *Early Christian Writings*, op cit, 109.
81 See *Catechism of the Catholic Church*, between #184 and #185.
82 Thomas Keating, *Open Mind, Open Heart*, Continuum, 1986/2008, 121–122.
83 At the beginning of John Main, *The Way of Unknowing: Expanding Spiritual Horizons Through Meditation*, Canterbury, 2011.

64 A Friendly Guide to Prayer

www.ingramcontent.com/pod-product-compliance
Lightning Source LLC
Chambersburg PA
CBHW042239180426
43199CB00040B/2931